M000285256

UNMISTAKABLY OLD

And doing pretty well, considering....

Ann G. Thomas, Ed.D.

From the long running newspaper column of the same name

Good for a laugh or two. Love, Ginny

Copyright © 2016 Ann G. Thomas, Ed.D.

ISBN: 978-1-63491-094-1

All rights reserved. No part of this publication may be reproduced, stored in a retrieval system, or transmitted in any form or by any means, electronic, mechanical, recording or otherwise, without the prior written permission of the author.

Published by BookLocker.com, Inc., Bradenton, Florida, U.S.A.

Printed on acid-free paper.

The characters and events in this book are fictitious. Any similarity to real persons, living or dead, is coincidental and not intended by the author.

BookLocker.com, Inc.
2016

First Edition

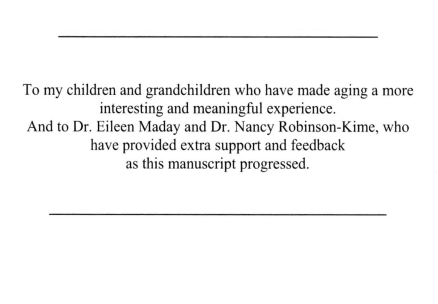

To my children and grandchildren who have made aging a more
interesting and meaningful experience.
And to Dr. Eileen Maday and Dr. Nancy Robinson-Kime, who
have provided extra support and feedback
as this manuscript progressed.

TABLE OF CONTENTS

INTRODUCTION OH MY!... 1

I. CHANGE.. 3

    MY NEIGHBORHOOD BANK..5
    CHOICES..8
    MEDICINE TODAY... 11
    THERE'S NO ONE THERE.. 13
    STOP BEING HELPFUL.. 16
    ANOTHER BANK STORY... 19
    TELEVISION COMMERCIALS.. 22

II. AGING 25

    AGE APPROPRIATE BEHAVIORS 27
    UNMENTIONABLES 29
    FORGETTING... 31
    WHAT WAS I THINKING? 33
    WHOSE BODY IS THIS?.. 35
    SHOPPING FOR CLOTHES 38
    THE FUTURE... 40

III. FAMILY 43

    BABYSITTING... 45
    THE DROP-IN GUEST.. 47
    EATING OUT 49
    THE BANK 51
    FAMILY REUNION 53
    THE FAMILY 55
    SUMMER JOBS... 58
    TODAY'S CHILDREN AND COMPARATIVE
        ADJECTIVES 61

IV. HOLIDAYS **65**

SANTA CLAUS 67
MERRY CHRISTMAS TO JUST US 70
PRESENTS 73
FAMILY THANKSGIVING 75
TURKEY GANGS 78
PRESIDENT'S DAY 81
MY HOLIDAY PARTY 84
CHRISTMAS CHANGE 86
THANKSGIVING 89

V. TECHNOLOGY **91**

APPS 93
EMAIL OPPORTUNITIES 96
FRIENDING 98
HI TECH WORLD 100
YELLING 102
GIVING UP THE CAR KEYS 104
TOILET PAPER 107

VI. CHANGING VALUES **111**

TAKING CLASSES 113
THE GYM 115
HOARDERS 118
HAVING WORK DONE 121
FOREVER YOUNG 123
WHAT'S IN A NAME? 125

VII. RELATIONSHIPS **127**

UNFINISHED BUSINESS 129
BEING HIT-ON 132
PUD 135

COUGARS...138
THE "S" WORD..141

INTRODUCTION
OH MY!

"We're down the rabbit hole with Alice. And the young ask, Do you think at your age it is right?"
An Unmistakably Old Woman

A funny thing happened on my way to *now*. I became *old*.

Not *old enough,* a magical age when one is able to get a driver's license. *Old enough* was celebrated.

Not older, a time in life dressed in responsibility. *Older* was the era of kids, jobs, and wrinkle cream.

Not *mature active adult,* the age of free time when we were encouraged to live differently from our work years. "Still young" we told each other as we volunteered and explored hobbies.

And after *mature*? That next stage is *old---Unmistakably Old*.

Here there are no models of behavior. There are no rules. It's true others have been this old before us. But the world has changed. To be *Unmistakably Old* in this century is to invent life as we go. We have left behind Dick Tracy with his watch and Maxwell Smart with his shoe phone. We are living yesterday's science fiction, writing the script as we go. The following is one woman's script. She identifies herself as *Unmistakably Old.* Her philosophy? *"Aging is an engine in motion. A drop of humor is the oil that keeps it going."*

UNMISTAKABLY OLD

I. CHANGE

"We're told change is the same as progress. Don't believe it. They are two separate things and only occasionally collide."

An Unmistakably Old Woman

1. MY NEIGHBORHOOD BANK
2. CHOICES
3. MEDICINE TODAY
4. THERE'S NO ONE THERE
5. STOP BEING HELPFUL
6. ANOTHER BANK STORY
7. TELEVISION COMMERCIALS

MY NEIGHBORHOOD BANK

Things in my community are changing faster than I am. Each week I make a deposit at my bank, and then cash a small check. The check is enough to cover breakfast with my friend and maybe a coffee or two, but it's not what anyone would call *living on the edge.* With such predictable behavior, there was no way I could have expected a problem.

Yesterday when I arrived at the bank, I noticed the tellers were all very young looking, and today wasn't *Take Your Child To Work* day. There was not one familiar person in sight.

A boy with a shaved head and an eyebrow ring waited on me. His nametag said Kevin.

I handed him my deposit, waited for a receipt, and then gave him my $30 check, made out to cash.

Kevin stood, looking at the check with all the intensity of one examining a ransom note. After a long moment, he looked at me, focusing toward my left ear. "Do you have any identification?"

"Excuse me?"

"Do you have any identification?" His look shifted to my right ear.

"I noticed you've looked at my check."

He glanced at it again.

"The check has the same number on it as this deposit receipt. The one you just gave me," I added, in case he hadn't been paying attention. "If I were a crook, do you think I would deposit $500 and withdraw $30?"

He looked confused, but repeated, "Do you have any identification?"

"Kevin," I said, hoping patience and logic could sort this out, "Do you see my check is printed by your bank, includes my name and address, and says I'm a valued customer?"

He squinted before slowly raising his head. This time he focused on my chin. There was a mumbling quality to his voice as he said, "I don't know you, so I need some identification."

"Yes," I responded, "we don't know each other. Perhaps we never will. But I've been here since 1980, a year that occurred before you were born, which means you are the new person. Since I've been giving you money, perhaps I should ask you for some identification."

Kevin turned to call for the manager, who arrived and listened as Kevin explained the problem. Unlike Kevin, she did make eye contact. Her eyes were not friendly.

"It's a policy designed to protect you." Her words were measured- perhaps she thought I was a bit slow. "We need to see some identification before we give your money away."

I thought I'd try a different approach. "What have you done with the bank's staff?" I asked. "I've noticed they're missing."

"We are the staff," she answered in a strained voice. "If you'll show us some identification, we can give you your money." I knew she wanted a picture ID, but I wasn't giving in that easily. I pulled up my sweater sleeve.

"All right," I said in my best-resigned voice. "Here is my birthmark. No one else has one like it."

By now Kevin was trying not to laugh, and I thought I might grow to like him. After all, hair will grow back, and a person can learn eye contact. I was pretty sure, however, that Ms. Manager and I would never become friends.

"A birth mark is not a proper form of identification," she said.

"Of course it is," I responded. "The police use it all the time. I've seen it on television. Birth marks and dental records are standard ways of identifying people." By now Kevin was nodding in an affirming manner.

Ms. Manager sighed. "What about a PIN? We could identify you that way."

"Are you trying to trick an old lady?" I asked. "I think you may have the real bank staff locked up in the vault, and now you want my PIN! Absolutely not! Maybe you should give me back my deposit."

Ms. Manager took one final look at my account on the computer, and then said to Kevin, "Give her the $30."

"Thank you," I said. "Will you be here from now on so you'll be able to identify me?"

She was walking away at that point, but I swear I heard her mutter, "I hope not."

CHOICES

Decision-making has become more difficult. I've been reading about what happens with aging brain cells.

While I was wondering how serious my cell loss was, my niece called to say she and her husband and new twin babies were coming to visit. I put aside my wondering and left to shop for the necessary items.

First on my list were baby wipes. In my day we had baby washcloths. These were a smaller and softer version of an adult cloth. Those days are gone. Now they've been replaced by a disposable moistened wipe. That seems wasteful to me, but since this was a short visit, I was willing to go with the times – willing, that is, until I reached the drugstore aisle devoted to baby products.

Decision time: name brand vs. generic, original vs. new and improved, scented vs. unscented, lotion, aloe, or plain, quilted or smooth, original pack or refill, and small, medium or large?

Two little people relied on my making a good decision although I hoped the Food and Drug Administration had been vigilant in not allowing anything harmful in these products. Still there were questions.

Would either baby be allergic to a scent? Was generic a product of equal cleansing ability? In what way was the wipe improved? Did any product contain anything that in years to come might be found to be carcinogenic? Was aloe or lotion better for tender little bottoms?

The choices seemed clear: call my niece long distance, get a degree in chemistry, or close my eyes and point. I was ready to point when a young woman stopped in front of the baby wipes. She smiled, pulled a box off the shelf and moved on. I helped myself to the same brand. Probably her child is nothing like my niece's two little boys. But she looked like a kind, loving woman.

The young family planned to be here for breakfast the next morning. I had eggs and toast on hand, but needed to pick up some orange juice. Perhaps I was a bit tired after the drug store, but still, buying orange juice shouldn't be complicated.

Frozen or fresh? Concentrate or not? With or without added calcium or Vitamin D? High, low or no pulp?

Now I try not to say "I remember when" often, but I couldn't help myself. I remember when you bought oranges, put them in a squeezer and drank the damn stuff. An orange had whatever it came with, and anyone who wanted more calcium drank a glass of milk.

The feeling of being overwhelmed was growing. I was getting less tolerant and more irritable. It was time for food. I went to meet my friend Mildred for an early supper.

"Burger and coffee," I said to the waitress.

"Would you like the Senior Menu burger or regular?" she asked.

"Regular please."

"Beef, turkey or vegetarian?"

"Beef."

"Quarter, third, or half-pounder?"

"Quarter."

"Medium or well-done?"

"Medium."

"With or without cheese?"

"Without."

"Tomato, onion and lettuce?"

"Please."

"Catsup and mustard?"

"Yes."

"Toasted or plain?"

A blank look.
"Your hamburger bun. Would you like it toasted or plain?"
"Plain."
"Fries, fruit, or coleslaw?"
"Fruit."
"Decaf or regular?"
"Excuse me?"
"Your coffee. Decaf or regular?"
"Decaf."
"Cream and sugar?"
"Black."
"And would you like to order desert now. I can tell you the desert choices if you'd like."

It finally hit me. My brain is fine. Enough of my little cells are doing what they've always done. I'm overwhelmed because there are too many choices. There are so many types of cereal that my grocery store has divided them into adult and family shelves although everyone knows family means sugar laden for children. A hamburger is beef, turkey, vegetarian or even buffalo or ostrich. It seems everything has an alternative.

All I can say is thank God I'm through menopause. Have you looked at the choice of products on that aisle lately?

MEDICINE TODAY

My grandmother enjoyed life into her late 80's with the help of Dr. Perry and his black leather bag. These days my friends and I need an army of specialists to keep us going.

The first stop is always the Primary Care Physician who has replaced Dr. Perry. This PCP is our first line of defense and the ticket booth to allow us to pass GO. My PCP does not own a black leather bag.

A long line of parts specialists and repair people are possible *next steps*. Each has an arsenal of tools at their disposal, complements of technology and modern chemistry.

Dr. Perry had the stethoscope, another little thing with a light so he could look into your ears and down your throat, a rubber tipped hammer to see if your leg would jump when he hit your knee, his knowledge and experience. That was it! Of course there were x-ray machines, but only a few. X-ray was needed if you fell down and broke something, or wanted to buy a pair of shoes.

I was a big fan of the x-ray machines in the shoe departments. Those machines were the final arbiter of a correct fit, used after the foot measure, the toe poking by both the sales person and your parent, and the walk around the chairs, staying carefully on the carpet. Then and only then were you directed to step up and place your feet in the *opening*. The bones of each toe glowed on the screen.

Now we understand x-rays can have serious side effects. Once word got out, bouff, the child-amusing shoe machines were gone.

Technology is changing medicine in many ways these days. I suppose that's good. It's happening whether I like it or not. X-ray machines of today look like small computers, except for the huge one designed to turn boobs into Panini without the grill marks.

But there is a down side. Have you noticed how impersonal medicine has become? It seems the idea of a bedside manner being an asset has disappeared. This is what happened during a visit to my PCP last week.

My doctor arrived in the tiny room where I was waiting. He smiled, glanced at my chart on his computer to remember my name, and inquired about my health. As I talked, he jotted notes on his laptop.

We were barely into my symptoms when some pleasant young thing from the front desk knocked on the door. That was the signal for him to hit the computer save button and print out a prescription. Then he stood, picked up the laptop, patted my shoulder, and with a smile rivaling Loretta Young, sailed out the door to the next eleven-minute encounter.

As for me, when the doctor walked out, the only thing I was left to gather were my thoughts since he didn't even ask me to take off my clothes. After one of those visits I like to take my car in for a check-up. My mechanic is willing to spend a much longer time chatting.

THERE'S NO ONE THERE

I don't pretend to understand the logic of the business world. But I've always believed the people who work for any company I do business with will be available if I need help. No longer is that true. One company after another appears to have replaced their Customer Service Department staff with disembodied voices.

My most recent interaction with a company's disembodied voice occurred when an unordered nationally known newspaper appeared at my door. Actually it was thrown onto my driveway. A mistake I thought until I discovered it came with a little address sticker with my name.

Perhaps a trial offer? After a ten-day-introduction the paper will go away, I told myself. I was wrong.

"Are you being billed for the paper?" a grandchild asked.

"No. At least I haven't seen a bill so far."

"If the paper is free," she continued, "why do you care? I've heard papers don't make their money from subscribers. They want readers—the larger the readership, the easier it is to sell advertising which is how they make their money."

There was a chance the grandchild was right. Her logic made sense, and I thought I had heard the same thing. Still, I didn't want the responsibility of going out in my bathrobe every morning in the rain or snow to retrieve the paper before it blew all over the neighborhood.

So I did what I thought would be a simple next step. I called to cancel. I believed, since this paper has been in circulation for years, they must have a phone number for their subscription desk, and a way to talk with someone. I was half right. Their subscription department was listed in the paper as an 800 number, which, now that I'm on a fixed income, I appreciate.

The 800 number, however, led to a disembodied voice offering a series of seven choices, one of which was for starting and/or stopping a subscription. That sounded right. I pushed the number, only to have eight new choices, leading me through another smorgasbord. Eventually I reached a voice instructing me to enter my numerical zip code, followed by a number appearing on the address label.

Next I was instructed to push 2 if I wanted to cancel or suspend the subscription. I pushed the requested 2 although I was a bit worried. I've always understood the word suspend to have a temporary flavor. I wanted the cancel choice, but there didn't seem any way to let them know, so I had to hope for the best.

It had taken me 42 minutes to conduct this two-minute transaction, but I guess the paper felt they had handled the situation in an efficient and frugal manner. After all, I was the only actual person who was involved. My subscription did stop, but resumed after a week, letting me know the *voice* had by-passed cancel in favor of suspend.

I'm not picking on this newspaper or their distributor, however. The no *customer-service* employees rule appears to be widespread. Everywhere I call, I encounter a message blocking access to a real person. Most of these messages also give multiple options. The ones I like best are the ones instructing me to *Listen carefully to the following choices because they have been recently changed.* Whenever I hear that message I wonder how many callers memorized the previous list of nine options and would push a wrong button if they weren't *listening carefully.* Since the options are all new to me, I pay close attention, push the button sounding closest to what I had in mind when I decided to call and hear, *Please hold. We are experiencing a high volume of calls, but will be with you shortly.* I hold,

and hold,
and hold
until I hear a click and a different recorded voice comes on
to say, *If you would like to make a call, please hang up and try
again.*

Frustrated, I began to explore my other options and decide
writing a letter may be a better idea. As I'm writing the phone
rings. A real person I've never met is on the line, calling me by
my first name or asking to speak to my long deceased husband
in order to sell us something I neither want nor need. So far I'm
not upset by these sales calls. I'm hopeful someone from the
newspaper will give me a call. "No thank you," I say. "But do
you by any chance know who delivers newspapers in my
neighborhood?" No luck so far, but at least it's good to know
some real people are employed somewhere.

STOP BEING HELPFUL

I believe most people mean well. A lot of those well meaning people are working to invent and change and update and (they think) improve those things we use in our everyday life. I wish they'd stop. They could begin with the telephone. Do you remember MA BELL?

They said she was a monopoly and we'd be much better off if anyone and everyone could get into the communication game. As far as I'm concerned, that idea was the kick-off for disaster. I know you remember the progression.

A phone was first a wall unit, and then a compact black thing that sat on a table or even a special chair. The phone was wired in to a *jack,* which attached it from your wall to "out there."

On the front of this black thing was a little movable circle with letters and numbers. Spinning this circle was called dialing. Dialing connected you to "out there". There was also a helpful woman who answered when you dialed zero. If the phone broke, the company would bring you a new one.

Over the years there was a progression from the basic dial phone to phones with buttons to push. Next someone figured how to allow the receiver to function detached from the base. Phones were now in color, which helped us think of them as part of our interior design plan, although since they detached from the base they were often lost in sofa cushions of a different and clashing color.

Of course we missed warning signs along the way. Instead of protesting, most of us embraced these changes, even experiencing a bit of envy when a friend was able to install a phone in his car. These changes occurred slowly enough that we failed to recognize we were headed toward technology hell.

But here we are. We wear a phone on our wrist that will also function as a heart monitor. The phone in our pocket takes pictures, sends mail, plays music and answers questions. Our computer phone has photo capabilities and will also locate a missing cell phone. And a button on the steering wheel of our car will recommend restaurants and call to make reservations.

And while there are a lot of people who will point out the advantages of these changes, there is another side, filled with what some people might consider drawbacks. Here are some.

- I forgot to charge my phone's battery so it's useless!
  MA BELLS phones didn't need charging.

- I can never find my phone!
  MA BELL had the phone attached to the wall so it was always where I left it.

- The keyboard is too small for my fingers!
  MA BELL's rotary phones were finger size.

- My phone doesn't work in some places and they tell me there aren't enough towers, whatever that means.
  MA BELL phones worked everywhere.

- Someone updates the phone model just when I've finally figured out what to do. At that point I need to start over. It's always a steep learning curve.
  Once someone knew the necessary phone number with MA BELL, there was nothing more to learn. If you didn't know the number, a woman named Information would help you.

- I have to buy the phone, learn how to program it and still pay a monthly charge.
  MA BELL's phone equipment was free.

- I'm never away from the office.
  When you walked away and closed the door, MA BELL stayed on your desk and waited.

And todays generation of young people never know the fun of making silly phone calls because these days the recipient can see your name and number before ever answering. (Remember games like "Is your refrigerator running? Better go catch it!)?

Last week a group of us were discussing meaning of life issues. Maria said, "Well, we know nothing leaves the universe."

I've been thinking about that idea and here's my question. If nothing leaves, where in the universe is MA BELL and can we convince her to come back?

ANOTHER BANK STORY

"Now what?"

This was from my friend Mildred who was having a cranky morning. We were eating a late breakfast so I knew it was just blood sugar impatience and nothing serious. I waited while she wrapped a piece of limp toast around one of her bacon strips and took a big bite before I continued.

"My bank has "greeters.""

She kept chewing.

"Do you have any idea what a bank pays someone to be a greeter?"

She took another bite while she shook her head "no". Then, with food in her mouth she said, "How much?" although it sounded like "Haw mooch?"

"I have no idea, but it has to be a huge waste of money. I went in to cash a check last week and this woman jumped out at me from behind a column. Scared me half to death."

"Why did she jump out? Maybe she was leaving or something."

"No. She worked there. She looked at me, smiled a big artificial looking smile and said '*Welcome.*' I almost wet my pants."

"Well, that doesn't sound so bad. She was probably trying to be nice."

"It's not nice to scare people, and it's not nice to pay people to do useless things."

"Did she say anything else?"

"When I left she said 'thank you for banking with us'."

"Well, she sounds pleasant. Maybe she just thought you needed a bit of friendliness. Did the waitress bring the extra butter?"

Mildred eats too much butter. I wanted to continue my bank story so I skipped my usual lecture and pointed to the dish behind her coffee cup.

"This bank pleasantness is becoming wide-spread. I heard a commercial on the car radio. Some man was saying he had to change banks because his bank was too small and couldn't meet all his banking needs. I spent a lot of time that afternoon trying to figure what kind of needs would be beyond the scope of a local bank. In the commercial he decides to go to this other bank and when he got there some woman said *Welcome*, and chats with him about how wonderful her bank is. Finally she gave him cookies."

"Maybe she was a girl scout," Mildred suggested. "I always like girl scout cookies."

"Keep eating," I suggested. "You're missing my point. The commercial was clear. This woman was a bank employee. If you or I went to that bank, we'd be given cookies as well."

"When?"

"When what?"

"When are we going?"

"Mildred, pay attention. For all we know, this may be the beginning of a problem at the national level. First banks wasted our money in some kind of housing loan program. Then the government gave them all kinds of money for something called a bailout. And now they're spending the money on greeters and cookies."

Mildred poured some catsup on her scrambled eggs as she thought about what I was pointing out. "What do you think they should do with the money instead?"

Clearly the food had kicked in and Mildred was back to her supportive and practical self. We finished breakfast discussing ideas. Now I have to figure how to let the bank know our suggestions. I'm going to start with the cookie lady. Wish me luck.

TELEVISION COMMERCIALS

"I don't understand television commercials," I said to my friend Mildred. We were at our weekly breakfast get-together. "I know companies spend a lot of money, but what's the point?"

"They want to sell you something," she responded. "To do that, they need to show you how their product will benefit you." There was a spot of jelly on her chin, which I pointed to before I suggested I was no longer convinced that *helping* was the point.

"Drug commercials are a good example," I said. "I can remember when a radio announcer informed the listener that a particular laxative provided gentle relief, or a mentholated chest rub was good for congestion. They never mentioned their products could kill you. Now I'm told some advertised drug with a name I can't pronounce will help me with some physical issue I didn't know I had, BUT, in all probability, will also cause me breathing problems, skin rash, cancer, heart attack and bad breath."

"I think the companies are trying to look out for us," Mildred said, before taking another bite of toast, this time without jelly.

To tell you the truth, I was a little concerned with her response. Mildred is about my age, meaning Unmistakably Old, but I've never though of her as naïve, especially because she survived raising five boys.

"Well," I answered, "those same companies have to know America's children are struggling with weight and health issues, but they advertise a lot of junk food, which doesn't sound very caring to me."

She kept chewing.

"Companies also seem to put out a lot of commercials showing stupid stuff."

She nodded, which generally means she knows I'm on a roll and it's easier to be patient and let me get it out of my system.

"This weekend I saw some people rolling out of a moving car to avoid sharing their appetizer. I don't remember what the product was, but I can't imagine any food that would motivate me to exit a car in motion. That same evening I saw a truck going down the side of a snowy mountain like kids do on snowboards. Some idiot is going to try one or both of those things and get killed."

The waitress came by to refill our coffee cups. Mildred asked for more grape jelly. We waited while the waitress hunted on adjacent tables for grape. When she left, Mildred struggled to open the little container. Her arthritis creates problems, in spite of her medication, --medication prescribed by her doctor, not some actor on TV.

"The one that gets me, really gets me," I continued, "is the drug that helps men with ED."

"Which one," she asked.

"The one that gives you a long time on the same pill."

"So why is that a problem? Seems like that would please both parties."

"It's not the time issue," I answered, "although going at it for four hours seems to me excessive, especially because the experience apparently may need to end with a phone call to a doctor. The ad doesn't mention which partner will need the doctor's assistance. But here's the part I can't figure. Every one of those commercials start with a look or gentle touch and end with the man and woman each sitting in their individual claw-foot bathtubs in some outdoors place. That makes no sense."

I broke off a piece of my bagel, spread some cream cheese and the two of us sat, chewing and thinking, or maybe just remembering. Mildred broke the silence.

"Maybe the tubs come out after four hours and what we can't see is what's inside."

We thought about that for a few minutes. Then, "Well, what do you think?"

"Could be warm water. They're relaxing," she suggested.

"Or could be cold water to cool them off."

And then it dawned on me. There's probably no way to know, but here's what I think. There is nothing in those tubs. The ad company wants to create an ambiguous image that will cause people to remember their product.

And guess what? It worked.

II. AGING

"The only way to become the type of old person you want to be is to start early. Old people are simply exaggerations of the person they've always been."
An Unmistakably Old Woman

1. AGE APPROPRIATE BEHAVIORS
2. UNMENTIONABLES
3. FORGETTING
4. WHAT WAS I THINKING?
5. WHOSE BODY IS THIS?
6. SHOPPING FOR CLOTHES
7. THE FUTURE

AGE APPROPRIATE BEHAVIORS

As an Unmistakably Old woman with a very large family, I know many educators, psychologists and know-it-alls who sometimes talk about *"age appropriate"* behaviors. It seems collecting baseball cards becomes age appropriate somewhere in elementary school. Boys calling girls stupid is age appropriate around the ages of eight to ten, but not when they're men. I began to wonder what would be considered age appropriate behavior for someone who is Unmistakably Old. Here is a short list, which I'm sure you can expand.

#1: Shoes--actually purchasing and wearing *ugly* shoes. Younger people may think we don't know the shoes on our feet are ugly. We know. We don't care! A moment occurs when comfort edges ahead of appearance. Comfort, with footwear means solid, sturdy, low to the ground, and outstandingly unattractive. Comfortable shoes are restricted to basic shoe colors. Fashion colors would be too conspicuous.

#2. Doctors-- lots of doctors. Younger people tend to have one or two doctors whom they see infrequently, unless they are reproducing or have survived combat. On the other hand, we Unmistakably Old have many. And we visit them all. There is the gerontologist who refers us to the specialist of the month. There is the cardiologist, the podiatrist, the dentist, the dental surgeon, the optometrist, the urologist, the neurologist, the rheumatologist, the chiropractor, and the dermatologist. Those of us who live in California, probably see an acupuncturist, a psychologist, and an herbalist as well. This small army serves to keep us healthy. Keeping up with this scheduling also exercises our minds.

#3.Timing—a need to be early. We like to eat early which has given rise to the Early Bird Specials, a restaurant gathering of almost exclusively *cotton-tops*. We also like getting to the airport early, a phenomenon that has caused many of us to lie to our adult children about the time of our flight to avoid ridicule.

#4. Speed—going from zero to sixty. Not our car. Us! Although it seems bizarre, this urge appears whenever there is the chance of being at the front of a line. No matter how long it took us to fill our grocery cart, or how many aisles we blocked as we pondered the merits of various soup brands, once we near checkout and see an open checker, watch out! Our nostrils flare, our hearts pump, and we begin our move, zigging, zagging, darting and ducking. Once there, however, we are again in no rush. We slowly unload our cart, inquire about the checker's health, search the side display for the right roll of mints, and rummage around in the bottom of our purse for exact change, using that opportunity to get rid of all those pennies no one else seems to want these days.

#5 Noises-- spontaneously emerging from various parts of our body. A snort seems to blasts forth the moment I drift off to sleep during an afternoon nap. A strange sound emerges when I bend over, resembling, as close as I can determine, a yawning hippo.

Now some people maintain most of these age appropriate behaviors are unpleasant or embarrassing or both, but I beg to differ. One of my grandchildren has green hair. That is embarrassing. A granddaughter has PMS. That is unpleasant. At my age, well what can I say? I'm just being age appropriate.

UNMENTIONABLES

There are a lot of *unmentionables* when it comes to old people.

For example-chins. Old people seem to lose them. I imagine there is a giant building somewhere filled with chins previously assigned to old people. Maybe there are even labels on the doors of various rooms: Pointed Chins, Squared Chins, Chins with small molds. I have no idea what becomes of all those chins. Perhaps plastic surgeons shop there.

While we're on the subject of chins, no one seems to mention hair on chins. Women's chins!

"So let me be sure I'm understanding you," one of my granddaughters says. "You're saying that when I become old the bottom part of my face will become a slope down to my collar bone with no discernible angle, and it will be covered in hair?"

"Probably not covered," I answer. "It's more like spaced hairs, as if each wants to be the center of attention. But don't worry. No one will say anything."

"I don't want to grow more hair," she moans.

I hasten to reassure her. "Your body will compensate by losing it in other places."

She thinks this over for a moment before deciding hair loss isn't much of a secret. "After all," she tells me, "there are hair replacement ads on television, and a lot of people have wigs."

"Ah yes," I answer. "Hair loss on the head is obvious. But not *down there!*"

In fact, loss of hair in the *private* region may be more of a non-talked about issue then chins. After all, there are plastic surgeons willing to do face-lifts.

Wrinkles get a lot of attention, as does having difficulty walking, but they're mentioned because someone has a product to sell. Scooters are advertised on television. Shelves are filled with products promising to remove, reduce, or prevent wrinkles.

Mentioning those things isn't a problem, but what about arm flab? How many people talk about that? Trust me, it happens! At some point those muscles previously on the underneath part of the upper arm quit working. Some old women exhibit either brave self-assurance or total unconsciousness by wearing sleeveless dresses, allowing the flab to bounce around with every move. Guess what! No one says a word.

Or loss of sexual desire? Television is peppered with ads for men who apparently suffer because of E D and we all know what that means. The ads even tell men how to talk about it. Ask your doctor, swallow a pill, and you're good for up to 36 hours. But what if his partner isn't interested? Many Unmistakably Old Women are, but many aren't. So far, no one mentions that.

Forgetting receives a lot of attention. Speaking out of turn, whatever that means, seems to be ignored. As a child I was often advised to *hold my tongue* but as an Unmistakably Old person I can be as outspoken as I like.

And how one behaves? Here is where the fun begins. Once one is Unmistakably Old it seems little will be mentioned. It's true I overheard one of my grandchildren questioning whether I was getting a tad *ditsy*. *Ditsy* is a term I've always thought was a psychological description, but my granddaughter, the one studying psychology, tells me it's not. That's good, because it seems whenever someone gets a psychological label, there is another pill to take. I'm taking enough pills, although it seems no one mentions those either.

FORGETTING

Now that I'm Unmistakably Old, I realize there are two kinds of forgetting. One is the everyday variety, which increases with age and gives rise to questions like *Why did I come into this room?*

My friend Betty has a severe case of the everyday variety. This might be concerning if it were new, but we've been friends since our children were little and she's always been forgetful. We called her a *space cadet* until we realized if the space program acted this way, they would be landing the capsule in Boston.

Now we take turns reminding her of meetings and appointments and watch to make sure her children don't put her in a Nursing Home. Her older daughter is still upset about those times Betty forgot to pick her up from school.

The beginning of dementia is the second type. I always thought dementia occurred like a lightning strike and, like lightening, there was nothing one could do. The *"it couldn't happen to me"* philosophy worked fine until I read a recent article.

The author seemed excited with his theory that exercise could head off forgetfulness. "The effective exercise," he wrote, "is mental. We should think more, and the most effective type of thinking is problem solving." If I understand his theory correctly, having a lot of problems in life, although bad for one's health because it creates stress, is good for one's mind. On the chance he's correct I try to make sure I think every day.

However, thinking isn't always easy to document. I mean a push-up is a push-up, able to be seen and counted. How does one see or count thoughts? I always thought I was thinking. Now I wonder. Does wondering count?

As I try to sort this out, I realize there might be an upside to forgetting. First, it frees one up for unplanned and unexpected situations. For example, yesterday I forgot why I had gone out to the back porch, which then freed me to look around and see what I'd like to do. As it turned out, there was a lovely breeze and I had almost a half-hour of enjoying the view of the garden before I remembered I needed to water the porch plants. I'm having a bit of trouble deciding how not to worry about what I'm supposed to be doing, but I tell myself, that's good so long as worrying qualifies as problem solving.

Second, forgetting provides an excuse to get out of doing something unpleasant. Yesterday I forgot to call my cousin Hattie, the family complainer. I'm between a rock and a hard place with this one. Calling is annoying, but not calling produces guilt. Cousin Hattie relies on guilt, but this is exactly where forgetting can be handy. I usually call on Friday mornings but yesterday it was too late by the time I remembered. Now I can only hope Hattie's forgotten.

I did slip and tell my granddaughter I'd discovered some benefits of forgetting. She's the granddaughter who's studying psychology, and you won't believe what she told me. She said, "Really, Grandma, at your age why do you need an excuse to do what you want?"

I'm still thinking about her question. Until I find a good answer, I'm also thinking about what I want for dinner.

WHAT WAS I THINKING?

Wouldn't you think, once a person becomes Unmistakably Old, they would have learned not to make a fool of themselves? It seems to me, with all the liabilities that come with age, the Universe should, at the very least, protect us from *egg on the face.* Maybe there are older people who are able to conduct themselves with decorum. I don't seem to be in the group.

About a month ago, for example, I fell off the curb in front of the post office. My first response, once I hit the parking lot asphalt, was to look around, hoping no one had observed my ungraceful act. Wouldn't you know? About seven people rushed to help me.

"What happened?" someone asked. To this day I can't explain my answer. I heard myself say, "I must have been pushed."

Immediately three people backed away, leading me to believe they had a history of pushing people and didn't want to be implicated.

A woman asked if I had broken anything, although why she would trust my response was beyond me. I smiled, said I was fine, and let her help me to my feet so I could limp, with whatever dignity I could muster, to my car. Once there I suddenly had a new thought—this time about my underwear. I was sure, when I got home and looked, I would find holes in my underpants and at least seven people now knew that I was not only a clumsy, wacky old woman, but slovenly as well. I spent the evening trying to decide which of those characteristics was most embarrassing. I had the time to think. It was off-season. There was nothing good on television.

I'm often surprised by what body parts no longer work although my children seem to think I should know. Last Thursday I found myself on my knees in the garden wondering if any of the weeds I'd been pulling would be safe to chew on to sustain life if I couldn't figure how to get myself into an upright position before dinner. Fortunately one of my daughters arrived before dark. Unfortunately it was the daughter who had told me the week before to stop doing chores involving getting up and down. All she said was, "What were you thinking?"

There is a series of other "little mistakes" I can't explain, even to myself. Recently I decided to color my hair. Now I know enough not to try the product that turns you blue, but I've always liked black. The gorgeous woman on the drug store shelf's box stared back at me. I couldn't wait to turn my hair the color she was illustrating. Three hours later when I finally looked in the mirror to view the finished product – well, what can I say? I've never seen an Unmistakably Old hooker, but I swear I now know what they must look like. It's not a pretty picture.

In thinking about this, I've decided that the only way to avoid an occasional embarrassing situation is to do little or nothing. But as far as I can tell, that's not a life worth living. So now I'm searching for a good answer when I'm asked what was I thinking. I'm debating between *It seemed like a good idea at the time* or *I didn't notice because I was solving the issue of world peace.* I'll let you know how this works out.

WHOSE BODY IS THIS?

Someone stole my body. It must have happened when I wasn't paying attention. Not only is my body missing, but an inferior one replaced it. This replacement body is old. Since I've never had an old body before, I have no idea what to expect. Does an ache or pain signal a problem? Or is that simply how an old body feels?

For example, vision became a problem when the phone company reduced the print size in phonebooks. The situation became worse when I called to complain. The customer service person actually denied they had done such a thing. I tried arguing, but finally gave up, and bought a pair of reading glasses, thinking this would resolve my vision problems. That same night I noticed the most beautiful ring around the moon, the type of ring I always heard referred to as a fairy ring. I phoned my son to go outside and look, but it wasn't visible from his house.

Several nights later when I was out for dinner with one of my daughters, I noticed each streetlight had a similar ring. This seemed a bit excessive so I decided to not say anything, and waited to see what would happen. What happened, of course, was that the phenomena beginning as fairy rings transformed somehow into cataracts. Having this type of information ahead of time might have helped, but I've seen no fairy-ring article in any magazine. Maybe AARP should look into this.

Soon after the episode with my eyes, a pain developed in my foot. "It's a gland," my Podiatrist informed me. "You've lost fat on the ball of your foot, removing normal protection around the gland."

Now really! I've spent almost my entire life in the battle against fat. Of all the places I've tried shedding pounds, my feet never even made the list. I was hoping the good news would be a weight loss but when I got on the scale, my weight had not decreased a bit. Clearly this particular fat wasn't lost. It simply relocated.

Speaking of relocation, hair is a leader here. While hair on one's head appears to thin, it is actually traveling to other places on the face and body. It's not uncommon to wake up and find a six-inch long hair has grown from the middle of one's neck during the night. If left alone, I have no idea how rapidly this neck hair would continue to grow. I suspect many elders who are found dead in their beds did not die of natural causes. Mutant hairs strangled them.

Skin is another issue. Gone are the days of smothering oneself with baby oil and lying in the sun to get golden brown. Apparently also gone are the days when you can simply sit outside in the sun. Now you need to wear sunscreen at various levels of protection, 20%, 40%, 50%, depending on how sunny it is. Who can decide? I don't know how to measure the intensity of the sun, so, when I remember, I wear the 50%.

There is also a choice of color in the sunscreen. I've tried both. The colored is dark enough to convince me I've overdone my base. The plain is ghost white. "Throw out that white stuff, Mother," a daughter advised. "You look like you've already died."

Now I'm being told there is another invisible problem. There is damage under the skin's surface; caused from how much sun I got as a child. Being in the sun now brings the damage to the surface in the form of spots. My dermatologist examines each new spot with her magnifying glass while reminding me "You don't want any more sun." Well, actually I no longer want the amount I've already gotten, but there doesn't seem to be any way to return the excess.

It would help if I had guidelines about how an old body is supposed to feel. Pediatricians say there is an age when teeth arrive. Is there an age when the teeth leave? If it is normal for bladder control to develop at a certain age, is it normal for one to lose it at another? I really wonder about that one when I notice today's drugstore shelves.

"I think I've figured something out," I said to Mildred at lunch yesterday. "You know how I'm always complaining about how much everyone talks about their aches and pains when they get old?'

She nodded.

"I think its because we're all in shock. We have what my granddaughter calls PTSD. The trauma is getting old."

Mildred sat without saying anything but I think the look she gave me was one of admiration. After all, I may have come up with something important. I plan to mention it to my granddaughter the next time we get together. I don't know if her psychology professors have considered this idea yet, but I'm always happy to share. Young people are very busy these days. They can't be expected to know everything.

SHOPPING FOR CLOTHES

Now that I've become Unmistakably Old, clothes are a problem. I'm never quite sure what to buy. What catches my fancy when I go shopping is often inappropriate, unflattering or downright ridiculous. And in case I don't notice, one of my descendants will be glad to point it out. They've been heard to say things like, "You don't plan to wear that, do you?"

Last week I was wandering around my local department store. I'd gone shopping for a baby gift. While I was having my purchase gift wrapped, I decided to do some shopping for myself. The hat department was close by and I remembered hearing hats were coming back. I grew up during a time when hats and gloves were a requirement for church, weddings, even downtown shopping. I was excited until I began trying them on. With each hat I checked the mirror and was faced with a new reality. Something had happened to my face. Over the years it had become a different shape. Every hat I tried was worse than the one before, causing me to have an immediate feeling of sisterhood with Queen Elizabeth who, everyone agrees, should leave the hats back at the palace.

I went from hats to casual wear. The mothers I knew growing up had two items qualifying as casual. One was an apron, put on as each meal was being prepared to cover the second casual outfit- a housedress. Times have changed.

The casual department was large, so I was optimistic. One can always use casual clothes, even though housedresses have disappeared. First I tried one of those cute mini skirts. They're coming back in style. The one I loved was a red plaid but the results were not good. It was clear gravity had done its work and a red mini should not accentuate what was left behind.

Next I noticed a section with a selection of slacks. Slacks have always been a good choice for me because of all they will

38

cover. Unfortunately something has happened to this season's selection. Many, it seems, have been cut on the bias, which accentuates the bulges. Hip huggers I didn't even try. After attempting to try on two sizes of straight leg jeans, both refusing to complete the journey up my legs no matter how hard I pulled, I decided I must be in the wrong department. I asked a clerk for direction to their department of fashionable casual clothing for old bodies. She suggested Goodwill.

Instead I headed to the shoe department. I used to love shoes, and to tell you the truth, I still do. The problem is they don't love me back. High heels don't work. Platform shoes leave me unsteady. Pointed toes are out. If a shoe doesn't fit just right there are going to be problems with my arch or my toes, or even my lower back.

However, all wasn't a total loss. I did find a pair of black sandals decorated with gold sequins. They will be perfect once warm weather arrives.

"You're not going to wear those," my oldest daughter said when I showed them to her. She's my rather uptight child, so when she objected, I knew I had picked out a winner. "You bet I am," I answered. "Even though I'm Unmistakably Old, I'm still here and *I can still make a statement!*"

She rolled her eyes.

THE FUTURE

Now that I'm Unmistakably Old I've begun to worry about the future. Not the immediate future. The future I'm worrying about is the one I'll arrive at once I'm dead. I began to think about this a few weeks back after our pastor delivered a sermon on the afterlife.

When I mention this new worry, friends tend to get religious on me, which misses my point. My faith is intact. The religious part doesn't worry me. It's the people! I've now lived so long that I know a lot of dead people. I'm worried about meeting some of them again.

I was explaining this to my friend Mildred when we met for lunch after church last Sunday. She and I go to different churches, which makes our conversations more interesting.

"I'm worrying about seeing my father again."

She gave me the arched eyebrow look without saying anything.

"He was a good dad."

The eyebrow stayed up.

"But he was only 39 when he died. I have a grandchild older then that. I can't imagine how in the world, I mean the other world, I'm supposed to relate to a father who's younger than my grandchild."

To her credit, and my gratitude, Mildred simply nodded, acknowledging this could present a problem.

"There's more," I said. "There's Paul."

"I thought your husband's name was Mac."

I nodded. "Paul was before."

"Did you…?"

"No, but I wanted to, and I never told my husband about Paul. I kept it a secret because…well, it was a memory I could pull out occasionally. And each time I did, the feelings came back, only better, because as I grow older and more experienced, my imagination becomes better."

"But, you never met up with Paul? And you loved Mac?"

"Never, and of course I loved Mac. Still do."

"Then I don't see the problem. Surely Mac will forgive you."

"But I don't want forgiveness. I worry it's not possible to have secrets in Heaven. I want to keep this a secret. Eternity is supposed to be a long time. Once Mac knows, I'm sure my feelings will disappear. Feelings are always stronger when they're secret. With so much time on my hands, I might want a moment or two with my fantasy."

Mildred shook her head.

"And…"

She waited.

"I'm also worried about Eleanor Roosevelt. Eleanor and Einstein.

Mildred was silently staring at me.

"No, not fantasies. It's just that they were so…so, well, the preacher said something about our all being equal in Heaven. Well, I started thinking, trying to imagine not feeling in awe of Eleanor Roosevelt or Einstein, or Becky Bennett."

"Becky?"

"You know, that beautiful, perfect girl in school who did everything right. Everyone has a Becky, although maybe she qualifies for the Unfinished Business category, because I still hope she grew up to be really ugly and dumb. Mildred was still quietly watching me.

"Well?" I finally asked.

"And you started worrying about this because of a sermon you heard a month ago?"

"It was a powerful sermon," I said.

"I can tell," she answered. "Let's order hot-fudge sundaes. I think your blood sugar is low. And next Sunday, maybe you should come to church with me."

III. FAMILY

"If your family's large enough, you get all kinds. The good news is that there's someone for everyone. The bad news is all the others."

An Unmistakably Old Woman

1. BABY SITTING
2. DROP-IN GUEST
3. EATING OUT
4. THE BANK
5. FAMILY REUNION
6. THE FAMILY
7. SUMMER JOBS
8. TODAYS CHILDREN AND
9. COMPARATIVE ADJECTIVES

BABYSITTING

As an Unmistakably Old Grandmother, I have become a designated baby-sitter. My family has a slew of kids. And it seems most of these children have parents who want to get away from them for an evening or weekend.

Now I adore children, especially ones who carry my genes. Having them around is fun most of the time. I have discovered, however--RULES are required.

My first rule concerns health. Knowingly dropping off an ill child without mentioning any illness, particularly when that illness involves bodily fluids is both sneaky and against my rules.

Should that happen, you are at risk. I will retaliate by giving your child some obnoxiously noisy toy, preferably one with a repeating song or animal noise. "The dog says woof, woof, woof" is only cute the first thirty times and the whine and roar of an interplanetary transport toy is guaranteed to drive you nuts. Leaving town will not work. I will track you down.

Rule number two concerns activity level. I will accept hyperactive children only if they don't expect me to participate. I will pitch a ball, but not run bases. I will sit in the shade at the pool, but will not play Marco Polo. I will go to playgrounds, batting cages, and Chuck E Cheese© only if your child is able to stay within sight, and doesn't expect me to climb, hit balls or eat pizza.

Rule number three concerns food. Teaching manners appears to be an old fashion idea in some of my descendants' homes. Perhaps this is the consequence of working parents. Or maybe times have changed. No matter! I remain committed to my values. When these children are grown and invited to dine with the Queen in London, they will remember what I've taught and won't disgrace the family. They will use utensils instead of fingers, chew with their mouth closed, wait to begin the meal until everyone is seated, and use a napkin. I'm tough.

My fourth rule has to do with ATTITUDE. I don't like it. I don't mind any emotion based on some reality, even though it may be immature. I don't flinch when a two-year-old says NO. That's what two-year-olds do. I don't cringe when a nine-year-old mutters about fairness and its lack. These are the expression of honest feelings that fit the maturity or immaturity of the child. But a *negative, sulking, dirty-look, don't even try to please me* stance strikes me like fingernails on a chalkboard. This is my exception to the age appropriate rule. Sighs, eyeball rolling, and hair tossing, accompanied by a slouching motion may be teen age-appropriate, but not around me. In these moments I can understand why this child's parents want to get away since I share the feeling. I hope they have enough money to hire sitters.

A friend whose granddaughter is going through the *attitude* stage told me the English have a plan. They send their children away to boarding school during the attitude years, bringing them home only for short visits so they don't forget what the children look like. When the children have reached eighteen or twenty, they are allowed home, presumably because they are now pleasant. I thought about suggesting to my family that we relocate to England, but decided it would be too expensive since there are so many of us to move. Besides, except for the occasional attitude, I'm happy.

One of my friends refuses to baby-sit with any of her grandchildren, which means she's missing out on a heck of a good time. One simply needs to have some rules. I've told her she's free to borrow mine.

THE DROP-IN GUEST

I've become the designated recipient for cousin Gwen's good deeds. She apparently has made a pact with God that she would never forsake me in my old age. I pray regularly that God will let her know she's under no obligation, but God appears to have a similar problem with Gwen. She doesn't listen.

When she visits, Gwen brings food. Never good food. Not once has there been chocolate cake or peach pie. Instead she brings things that are good *for* me.

Gwen also brings her dog. She read somewhere that dogs are good for old people – brings them out of depression. The thing is, I'm not depressed. Never have been and don't imagine I'm going to start now, although, if Gwen keeps visiting, I may change my mind.

I like dogs. In fact, I describe myself as an animal lover since I also like cats and I watch the animal channel on television. There are very few animals I don't like, although Gwen's dog has made that list. She is one of those little dogs that yips when irritated. Apparently she finds almost everything irritating.

As we visit, Gwen feeds the dog little pieces of whatever snack she has brought, all the while encouraging me to eat. My standard responses teeter on the tightrope of good manners. Once I suggested I didn't feel well enough to eat. --a mistake because her response was a flurry of attention lasting three days.

When I'm with Gwen, I have a great deal of difficulty thinking of what to say. We disagree on religion. We disagree on politics. She doesn't read, so a good discussion about a current book is out. She doesn't watch television – not even the animal channel. She hasn't seen a movie in years, has no hobbies, and plays no games. We don't seem to know many of the same people, even in the family. Our topics seem to be health – mine is fine, hers is problematic- and the weather. Unexpected rains, cold snaps, and drought conditions may be terrible for crops but good for conversation.

I've spent a lot of time trying to decrease the frequency of Gwen's visits. When she rings the bell, I've answered with an announcement that I was just about to go out, only to hear she'll be happy to accompany me. She brushes off my suggestions that I am expecting company, or simply don't want to visit.

Once I suggested Gwen go back to school – perhaps get a counseling degree. I thought that was a brilliant idea. Becoming a student would take up a lot of her time, leaving her with less time for me. Besides, she might learn to listen, develop some sensitivity or, at the very least, learn an accurate definition of depression. My suggestion fell on deaf ears.

Help came from an unexpected place. Telemarketers! While most of my friends complain about the uninvited calls, I am happy when the phone rings. "Yes," I say as Gwen and Yippy look on. "Humm," I add, listening intently as Yippy becomes restless and Gwen looks at her watch. "Can you tell me how that would work?" I question as Gwen fidgets and Yippy begins to wiggle. "Could you go over that again?" I ask as Gwen wiggles and Yippy fidgets. "Oh," I intone as Gwen stands, motioning she must leave. "Can you hold a minute?" I ask, covering the phone to say *goodbye* and *drive carefully*. While I have yet to buy anything from these friendly chatty people who phone, I do hope they keep calling. At least until I figure out another way to handle Gwen's visits.

EATING OUT

My grandchildren and I often eat out. Last week I experienced my first Sushi Bar, which is like a drugstore soda fountain except they serve raw fish instead of root beer floats. Now raw fish might sound unappetizing to some. The manager had obviously anticipated that reaction and purchased rectangles of green plastic grass that could be spread as decoration. The green plastic grass didn't help me much. But I didn't have any better idea so I kept quiet.

Behind the counter was a young man who prepared what you ordered. Preparing meant cutting two small rectangles from a large piece of fish and molding each across individual rectangles of rice. That was considered a dish. Each dish was ordered separately. This seemed slow to me. My granddaughter said it's food to linger over. I told her there didn't seem to be much choice.

My real shock came with the bill. The portions were small, the service was counter service, and the food was uncooked. Doesn't that suggest a small bottom line on the bill? I won't mention how much it was, but I can tell you, it wasn't cheap. Maybe plastic grass is expensive. Still, I'll go back because the food is good. Next time though, I'll have a snack first.

Another granddaughter invited me to go to another type of Japanese restaurant where people sit around three sides of a table watching the cook, who stands at the fourth side, preparing food on a grill built into the table. The idea of having your food cooked in front of you was fun. However, the young man who was cooking turned out to be a real show-off. He tossed the food around and flipped his knife in the air. The more people admired his antics, the sillier he got.

I have a great-grandson who acts the same way and the school wants to put him on drugs. They call it ADHD, which is a modern term for the kids we used to call *wiggle worms*. I wonder if the staff at my great-grandson's school knows about this particular career option for overactive boys.

Another evening I went with a grandson and his girlfriend to a Moroccan Restaurant. We sat on the floor on big pillows. I was a little apprehensive since I don't get up and down as easily as I used to. But I figured if old Moroccans could do it, so could I.

One thing amazed me about this restaurant. There were no utensils to eat with. None! People ate everything with their fingers-like one of my children years ago. Perhaps his father and I had been unfair, insisting, as we did, that he use his fork and spoon. He might have been Moroccan and arrived at our family by mistake.

Of course all my meals out aren't this exotic. One of my favorites is a hot dog. Not any hot dog. I love the kind you buy at the ballpark, and load up with everything including sauerkraut. This type of hot dog requires a cold beer. Another favorite is a barbecue, complete with white corn on the cob and fresh tomatoes, both picked from the garden minutes before dinner. This should be followed by big bowls of chocolate ice cream on a hot afternoon.

These are ordinary food. One of my daughters likes reminding me that beer is alcohol and I shouldn't drink, corn on the cob is hard on my teeth, and ice cream contains fat. But my love of hot dogs upsets her the most. She tells me they contain things neither of us can pronounce.

This is the same daughter who spent several of her younger years refusing to eat anything green. She doesn't remember that. And of course I don't remind her. I do worry a bit, however, that her selective memory might be caused by a deficit in some nutrient found only in hot dogs. I'm waiting for the research before I mention that possibility. With this daughter it always helps to have an ally with credentials.

THE BANK

My stockbroker granddaughter stopped by for advice.

"I want to get pregnant, and I need help selecting the father."

"Have you met someone?" I asked.

"No," she answered, "and I'm running out of time. My eggs are getting old."

That one sentence plummeted me down the rabbit hole into a world as strange as Alice's wonderland. According to my granddaughter, eggs are not created "as needed" unless one is a rabbit. Instead each baby girl arrives with a full basket and, similar to eggs in the supermarket, each is stamped with an expiration date.

"Here, look at these." She spread papers on the table. Each was labeled *PROFILE*, followed by a number. "These are the different donors," she said.

In my day the male contribution to a new life came from either a husband or an indiscretion. I always thought about that male person as honey or darling or even husband. Never once, even at the most intense minutes of childbirth, did I think of him as donor.

Things change, I told myself. My granddaughter and I discussed the various merits of hair color, professional orientation, hobbies and interests as if these were somehow determining factors in the outcome, while ignoring that most of our children have different interests and hobbies from their fathers. And none in our family have selected the same profession as dear old dad. A few have the same hair color. But there are fewer hair color choices available. The law of averages would work here. My granddaughter also raised the question of the donor's age although none was over thirty-nine. Besides, I can't believe sperm is also wear-dated. Look at all the old coots procreating these days!

The conversation seemed to be going well and then I must have blanked out. I know as well as the next person that sperm is found in sperm banks. But I couldn't picture it. I'm pretty sure there are none in my neighborhood. We have a Wells Fargo, and a Bank of America. We used to have a Savings and Loan, but of course that's a different matter entirely. I don't imagine sperm are loaned. I mean- there isn't any way to return it after one is finished, is there?

Since my granddaughter had PROFILES, I'm sure she knows where the bank is. I hoped she didn't ask me for any advice about what to say once she went inside. Perhaps there would be lines, like a regular bank. But I wasn't sure what she should ask for. A sperm? Two sperm? A cup of sperm? In my day we didn't have to worry about the amount.

While I was puzzling this in my mind, my granddaughter mentioned that, even though it was call a donation, in no way was donation to be construed as free. Quite the opposite! She was planning to pay what seemed to me as an enormous amount of money for a product whose properties were invisible and whose success was not covered by warranty. No Good House-keeping Seal of Approval here.

She finally decided number 33845 was the best match. I imagine she will soon be on her way to motherhood. Now our only problem is what he or she will call dad. I mean, Number 33845 is a pretty long name for a little one to say.

FAMILY REUNION

Summer is the time for watermelon and corn on the cob, swimming and picnics, vacations and family reunions. Although the big reunion doesn't happen every year, this year is IT! In a family the size of mine, we need a committee to plan and organize this event. I'm on the committee. I figure at my age I know as much or more about family business then anyone, and my presence would speed things along. It become clear only ten minutes into the meeting that speeding things along was not going to happen.

We held that meeting two weeks ago. I arrived with a list of what we needed to accomplish. I'm sure everyone already knew the list, but it's good to have things written down.

1. Names and addresses for each of us. (Necessary for inviting people and setting up the overnight arrangements.)

2 A location for the weekend that will accommodate everyone.

3 A date that will work for most people.

4 Activities, food, et cetera.

I add et cetera on any agenda I create because in any group someone will always say, "You forgot…" and I can say, "It's included in the et cetera."

The six of us on the committee took almost the entire afternoon to list the names of everyone we could think of. Because we didn't want to forget anyone, we then circulated the list to various relatives. Every person who read it added more names.

Although I consider myself up-to-date for someone my age, I was shocked at the frequency people in this family divorce, remarry, hook-up and hangout. And it seems many "ex" somebodies are still included in gatherings with their new children, while many new "hook-ups" arrive with several young ones of their own. A list I considered quite large and inclusive at 96 has grown into 204.

"They won't all come," a daughter reassures me. I'm not sure how I feel about that. What if the people none of us know come while our actual blood relatives have become someone else's hookup?

For location we came up with a near-by spot that rents accommodations. And many of us have extra rooms, sofas and spaces for tents. I thought location would produce arguments, but the bad economy helped. Any exotic location or resort was too pricy. The local people all said they were happy not to have to travel. The Out-of-towners wrote comments like, "We'll just pitch a tent in Cousin Sharon's yard."

We settled on a weekend in August. The August date won because it took us so long to settle on the list of who we were, that it wouldn't have been possible to gather everyone earlier.

As for activities, we now have a sub-committee working on those. I opted off that committee. What I want to do is sit around and talk to family members I haven't seen in a long time.

Most of the invitations were sent via email, which is a different dynamic than how it used to be. We're receiving acceptances at a rapid rate. A granddaughter and I were going over the replies yesterday, and making lists of who's connected to whom. We're stuck on identifying someone who answered the *"Are you coming?"* question with "You Bet!" And signed it " *Butch."* Butch wasn't on any of our original lists. No one we've asked knows of a Butch. So, if any of you know how Butch is related, would you please let me know?

Meanwhile, we need sign-ups for coolers and grills. See you in August.

THE FAMILY

I've begun to notice that my family is a bit of a disappointment. Maybe my expectations were off, but the family I've ended up with is not what I had in mind when I was young. I've been trying to figure out what went wrong and I've got a few ideas.

To begin with, some of my family members have no sense when it comes to picking out a mate. As a result, we've added some real duzzies over the years. What's made it worse is that they not only married these oddballs, but they reproduced with them, creating a new generation peppered with aliens. Don't get me wrong. I don't object to someone being different. In fact, I find difference interesting. If the in-laws in question had personalities that were an improvement, I'd even be excited. And I'm a realist, so I'd settle for an even exchange, but no such luck.

One of my sons married a woman with an overactive clean-gland. She's the type of woman people are talking about when they say, "You could eat off her floors." WHY? Even dogs get dishes.

And there's the nephew who rants and raves about "those damn kids." He objects to green hair, droopy pants, tattoos, and pierced body parts, and to tell the truth, I'm not fond of those things myself, but I believe perspective is called for, since they are, in fact, kids. I'm debating, the next time he starts on his monologue, whether I should point out to him that wearing one's trousers at half-mast below a beer belly or attempting to disguise his age with a comb-over lacks appeal. Probably I'm better off keeping quiet, but it's tempting.

It's difficult when some relative parades an unacceptable person in front of the rest of us and asks for an opinion. I remember saying on a couple of occasions things like, "You're joking, right?" or "Surely you can't be that desperate." For some reason these comments didn't go over too well and some of my young relatives got all prickly. That was when I realized the question, *What do you think?* has no room for multiple-choice answers. Now, if the person seems awful to me, I turn my head and mutter, "I'm feeling faint and need to sit." It's awkward when I'm already sitting.

Now don't get me wrong. Some of the married-in are terrific. In fact, one grandson managed to marry someone who is an improvement over anyone in the family, and I'm hopeful they will reproduce and improve the gene pool. We had another terrific marry-in on a second marriage, but it turned out he had all the kids he wanted during the first marriage and had gotten fixed.

I'm not sure about this idea of getting fixed. When I look at my own children, I notice some of them didn't turn out as well as I expected. In retrospect I think I made a wise decision to have a lot of kids. It was a way of playing the odds that worked in my favor. If I'd gotten fixed I would have stopped too soon, although I don't mention that to the older children.

I also find it upsetting how easy it is to divorce and what lousy criteria comes into play when deciding whether to keep someone or get rid of them. A grandson-in-law I thought was terrific is gone, while a son-in-law who has always been a pain is still around. I wish someone would consult me before they go running off to a lawyer because it's beyond me how these kids make that decision. One of my daughters tells me that you never know what things are like until you live with someone. Perhaps that's true, but from my vantage point it seems there is a tendency in the family to keep some rather boring individuals and get rid of several who were interesting if somewhat erratic. Frankly I think the idea of predictability is overrated. Because of that value we've lost a cowboy, (O.K., not easily employed in the city), a poet from Boise (yes, he drank, but not that much), and a male dancer (He understood the pink tutu was a mistake.)

My children are fond of saying to me, "You know mother, we're not the Waltons." I assume that's supposed to help me gain perspective, but I think they're missing the point. I never aspired to be the Waltons but I'd prefer not resembling so closely The Adams Family.

SUMMER JOBS

Summer is here! School is out! Some young people have looked for and secured jobs! And, as an Unmistakably Old member of this family, I've been satisfying my curiosity by asking about those jobs. I was secretly hoping we had the next technology genius in our family—someone like those boys who founded Apple. So far it doesn't look promising.

Instead, here's what I've found. Three grandchildren are lifeguards. That's a good job with the right mixture of social interaction and responsibility, and it allows parents to feel they're getting a bit of a return on their earlier investment in swimming lessons.

Two are away at camps - one as a counselor and one as something called CIT, which means counselor-in-training. Again we're seeing a return on investment, with the bonus of clean bedrooms for however long they're away.

Three are in the food industry—honest, that's what they call it. When I inquired for specifics, one busses tables, one waits tables, and one works in a fast food restaurant where I wouldn't even taste what is served.

The rest run the gamut of summer jobs. They pick fruit, baby sit, mow lawns, clean houses, stack grocery shelves—you know, all the usual jobs that didn't disappear like Soda Jerk. However, I did uncover something a bit weird that I'll share with you. The conversation went something like this.

ME: "Who are you working for this summer?"
GRANDSON (GS) "The water company."
ME: "What do you do?"
I hoped his job description didn't involve anything that had to do with plumbing since I was sure he knew nothing about such water related jobs as fixing a dripping faucet, loading and

starting dishwashers or flushing the toilet. He also never puts the seat down, but that's more a safety issue than a water problem. I know there are many people who don't know how to do the job they have, but I was hoping that vice would by-pass my family.

GS: "Count."

You're probably noticing this grandson is not the most verbal.

ME: "What do you count?"

Actually I was wondering what the water company needed to have counted in this age of technology. And why they would hire a teen with low grades in math, although I'm sure he did OK in elementary school where they taught counting.

GS: "Stuff. I count stuff and put it on a map they give me."

ME: "What kind of stuff?"

GS: "Water meters. Yeah, water meters and fire hydrants and manholes and storm drains. That's it. Just those things."

I promise you, this is the actual truth. At that point I stared at him for a long minute before I asked what I knew was an unproductive question.

ME: "Why?"

His turn to stare at me. Then

GS: "Why what?"

Accompanied by what I think was a shrug, although he might be developing a twitch.

ME: "Why do you count those things?"

GS: "Because they tell me too."

This was an awkward point to stop the conversation, since I clearly had very little information, but pursuing it further seemed to be pointless. My real concern now is the water company and I'm trying to decide what I need to do. How does a company responsible for the health and safety of such a large population lose their fire hydrants and storm drains? Why would a large company not even assume every house or building would have an attached water meter—they certainly know where the water meters are located each month when it's time to send the bill. And why, in this age of satellites and technology would they hire a teenage boy to walk around town counting those things? I did call to ask, but I think it was a summer job teen answering the phone and she had no idea. But if she needs a future job reference, I will say she was polite.

TODAY'S CHILDREN AND COMPARATIVE ADJECTIVES

My 9-year-old grandchild Billy won a trophy for basketball. I've seen Billy play, so I was surprised. At the two games I attended, Billy either sat on the sidelines or stood on the court looking puzzled while the other kids ran around and threw the ball at each other or sometimes at the hoop.

"Did you make the most baskets?" I asked when I saw the trophy. I was open to the idea that modern-day miracles might occur in sports.

Billy shook his head.

"Maybe blocked players on the other team?" I tried.

Another head shake.

"But your team ended up with the championship? Your team won the most games?"

"We didn't win any," he answered.

Wanting to make sure the trophy wasn't stolen I took a closer look.

There it was, engraved in bold letters, **The Red Hots,** and in slightly smaller letters, his name and the date. Nothing else. No indication of what he might have done to merit a trophy. Not even a mention of the sport.

Since it was obvious there was no further information available from Billy, I asked his mom.

"They give a trophy to every kid," she told me. "Children need to be encouraged."

Billy has always impressed me as an honest, reality-based child so I wasn't sure how this trophy-give-away was encouraging. I was beginning to wonder about the adults surrounding him.

"What do all these children understand about how a trophy signifies that someone wins and is best?" I asked her.

"They're all best," she answered. "These are the years to build self-esteem."

"What happens to the self-esteem of the child who was actually best?"

She stood looking puzzled which reminded me of Billy on the basketball court. Perhaps some things are genetic.

I could hear in my mind Miss Roberts in my own 5th grade class banging the yardstick on the chalkboard as she had us recite comparative adjectives: Good, better, best, was on her list.

A week later Billy and I were at a family picnic. Some of the kids were shooting baskets. Billy was hanging out in the shade with a book.

"How come you're not playing basket ball?" I asked.

"Don't like it," he answered.

"But you won a trophy," I persisted.

"They give those to all the kids," he answered.

"Why would they do that?"

Billy shrugged and went back to reading—clearly an activity he preferred over trying to explain adult behavior to his grandmother.

My granddaughter, the one who's studying psychology, overheard.

"Here's what I think, Grandma," she said. "Billy's self esteem seems okay to me, so his mom must be doing something right. I think the trophy give-away is connected somehow with the parent's issues—you know, unfinished stuff from their own childhood."

I think she's on to something. If I remember correctly, back in elementary school Billy's mom never made it into the *Cardinal* reading group and every kid, from the beginning of time, understood the *Cardinals* were the best. It didn't even matter if the teacher tried to change the names, renaming *Cardinals* as *Bluebirds* or even *Robins.* A *Cardinal* was *a*

Cardinal and they were the best readers. Good, better, best. It's a matter of comparative adjectives.

This issue, which I think I'll call *Trophy-Gate,* has taught me several things. First, we don't stop trying to heal our childhood "hurts" The psychologists may be right when they help people look backward to solve present day problems. I've also learned comparative adjectives are still alive and functioning, and finally, perhaps most importantly, a generic trophy is cheaper than a therapist. Now it remains to be seen if it's as effective.

IV. HOLIDAYS

"Do you know every day is designated to commemorate or celebrate something? I just discovered there is an <u>Old Stuff Day </u>and I'm wondering if that refers to me."

An Unmistakably Old Woman

1. SANTA CLAUS
2. MERRY CHRISTMAS TO JUST US
3. PRESENTS
4. FAMILY THANKSGIVIG
5. TURKEY GANGS
6. PRESIDENT'S DAY
7. MY HOLIDAY PARTY
8. CHRISTMAS CHANGE
9. THANKSGIVING

SANTA CLAUS

"Santa's gonna get sick and die."

"No he won't," someone responded.

"Yes. He's obese. We studied about food stuff in school, so I know!"

Those words, delivered by my granddaughter Elle with all the shrillness of a second-grader, managed to shut down the chatter at our recent family Christmas get together. Well, it shut down all but cousin Doris. We've never found anything that will shut her down once she gets going, although I think her husband would make someone a very rich person if they could figure that out.

We're a large family so there are a lot of us at any gathering, and most of us want to be helpful. One of the child's aunts, my oldest who seems to always have good answers, jumped right in.

"Santa's supposed to look like that because he's round and jolly. Remember how the story goes? 'He had a broad face and a little round belly'."

"That's obese. And it's even worse because he smokes."

"Not cigarettes," an older cousin added. It was unclear if his intent was to be helpful or get points for accuracy.

By now Elle was developing large eyes and a slightly reddened look -- a clear signal things were escalating.

My younger brother's wife, who is at least eighty pounds overweight and has several related health issues, patted Elle on the back. "A little extra weight doesn't mean he's going to die. That rule's about people who have hundreds of extra pounds."

At that point it was as if someone had sucked all the air out of the room. Everyone froze, watching *moving toward meltdown child* opposite *don't upset me with reality* woman. To Elle's credit, or perhaps to the credit of her parents, she didn't say what everyone in the room was thinking.

After about ten seconds that seemed like minutes, her dad said, "The story and those pictures are from a long time ago. I heard Santa went on a diet and lost a lot of weight, so I'm sure he's no longer overweight."

"He is." Five-year-old Kay was now joining the conversation. "I saw him yesterday, didn't I mommy?" She looked over at her mom who was unsuccessfully searching for a suitable distraction.

"He was still whatever you called it," Kay continued.

"Obese," Elle added. "Obese happens when people eat too much of the bad food, and not enough of their fruits and vegetables. The teacher said so."

"This rule about being overweight doesn't apply to Santa," someone offered.

"The teacher said it was the same for everyone. Everyone needs to eat the right food."

"I have a thyroid condition," someone near the hors d'oeuvre table said. I couldn't see who it was, but there were two possibilities, not that I'd be one to point fingers.

To tell you the truth, I was beginning to get a bit nervous. If things escalated too much, someone might let it slip that Santa was…well, you know. Elle's mom, jumped into the conversation.

"Well," she said, "I know the eating-right rule is for everyone, but here's what I think. I think Santa has some very strong magic. After all, he has reindeer that fly, and he and his elves make enough toys during the year for all the children in the world. I think, even though he probably eats some of the wrong food…"

"And smokes," Elle added.

"And smokes," her mother continued, "I think his magic makes him the one person where the rule doesn't apply."

Elle looked skeptical, but was clearly trying on this new idea to see if it was something she could live with.

"What did your teacher say about Santa and obesity?" Cousin Beth asked. Beth used to be a teacher before she retired and is always interested in the educational perspective.

"She said we should get out our workbooks 'cause it was time for math."

We don't pay our teachers enough.

MERRY CHRISTMAS TO JUST US

I belong to a group with seven other Unmistakably Old women. We started meeting five years ago; first as a book group because everywhere we went we were hearing other people talk about their book group and some of us felt left out. It didn't take long for the book group idea to fall apart. Two of the women never read, and didn't even own a library card. Although Nan volunteered to tell them about whatever we were reading, things fizzled. Becoming a book group was not our destiny.

Since we all to like to eat, I proposed we become a gourmet-cooking club. That idea failed to gain traction. My biggest supporter for that idea was Gladys and the more she talked, the more people remembered what a terrible cook she was.

During the next several months we tried one idea after another. We were "travelers" one month, fun until someone (I won't mention names) bought our bus tickets for the wrong night. Next we decided we'd go to a restaurant each month, but by the third month Dottie was on a health food kick and swore restaurants added bad things to their food that would shorten all our lives. That discussion became heated enough that Jean suggested shortening Dottie's life. Fortunately she said that under her breath.

We tried movies, crafts, cards, and TV and found nothing seemed to work for more than a time or two. We've now settled down to a bit of this and a bit of that.

Next of course was the decision about a group name. For months we thought if we could figure out the type of group we were, we'd have the name issue solved. We'd be "The Book Group" or "The Dining Out Group." When that didn't work, someone suggested "The Girls", but Mildred pointed out that Feminists might picket us since they disapproved of calling adult women girls.

"O.K." Peg said. "How about The Ladies?"

But that seemed to lack something as well. Now we call ourselves Just Us and it stuck.

Which brings us to this year's Just Us Christmas Party. Here are the rules for our gift exchange.

1. Select one of your possessions you'd like to get rid of. When the gift is opened, tell, if you remember, where the item came from and why you no longer want it.

2. Wrap the item in a way that doesn't give away what it is.

We will put all items on the table (under the tree would require repeated bending and in our group, bending leads to either a fall or a toot.)

We all draw numbers 1-8. Number one will select and open first. Number 2 either selects from the unopened presents or may take number 1's opened gift and give number 1 an unopened one from the pile. Once those two presents are unwrapped, number 3 may select from the pile or choose one of the opened presents. This continues until number eight, who has the choice of the one remaining wrapped present or any of the 7 opened ones. Once everything is open each person needs to explain her gift and convince the rest of us that getting rid of the gift was the right decision. The person with the best reason wins a box of chocolate covered pretzels.

It was a great activity that took hours, partly because we had to keep re-explaining the rules to Dottie. The presents were also pretty amazing. There was a hand-held can opener requiring a younger, non-arthritic hand to use, a gardenia scented candle, given by Jean who has almost no sense of smell, a wine glass from Estelle who has given up alcohol--well, you get the idea. But the best, the very best and winner of the pretzels was Jessica whose husband Herb left her twelve years ago to take up with his young secretary. Jessica brought, carefully wrapped in a used Macy's box, an 8X10 glossy of Herb. She couldn't remember where she got Herb, but it was obvious why she had selected the picture. Enjoy the pretzels, Jessica!

PRESENTS

I've told everyone to please stop giving me gifts. *There is nothing I need,* I say, but no one believes me. *It's just a little something,* are the words that accompany handkerchiefs, scarves, perfume, writing paper, bird feeders, playing cards, magnifying glasses, candle sticks, and a huge assortment of rusted things that are supposed to be for my garden. A granddaughter tells me, "Rust is the new look." This is the same granddaughter who pays a lot of money for furniture with chipped paint, so I'm not sure how much I can trust her judgment.

For many years I've stored these un-needed items in the bottom drawer of my dresser. The drawer was my own little store, and it worked well until a few years ago when it became so full it was difficult to open and close.

So I emptied a hall closet, and bought a spiral notebook. By the end of the day I'd moved everything from the drawer to the closet, and itemized each in the notebook, along with who sent it, and when.

The problem with this new system emerged over time with more presents coming in. Halloween brought a flurry of weird things, causing me to wonder why no one sends candy anymore. My cousin said it's because everyone thinks all old people are either diabetic or fat or both. Thanksgiving brought another deluge of presents, and what with writing all the thank-you notes I forgot to log the items into my book. Last Christmas was my opportunity to make progress. I happily pulled items from my closet, humming a holiday tune as I wrapped and addressed. My Christmas shopping was finished, thanks to my hall closet. Everything was wrapped, and mailed by the 10th. I had 15 carefree days to enjoy the season.

The first letter arrived on January 2nd.

"Do you realize that you gave me the handkerchief set that I sent you for your birthday?" she asked. During the next week there were five others who wrote to let me know they'd received the gift they'd sent me. There seemed to be only one way to handle the situation. I sent everyone the following letter.

Dear (whoever),

As many of you have noted, I sent presents this year that were, in many cases, ones you had sent me in the past. What some of you have suggested is true. I have a closet where I keep things to give to others. In the past, however, I have tried to send your lovely present to someone else rather than back to you. It seems my ability to continue doing so has eroded. Therefore, I am proposing the following: Buy me something you really like. Send me a card telling me what it is. Even better—for those of you who have one of the fancy phones, take a picture of the present and send that along. Keep the present. I will write my thank you and enclose a Christmas tag for you to attach, saying that the gift is for you, from me, with love. Since I need nothing, I will be happy you thought of me without having to re-gift something I can't use. You will have a gift you really like. We will have saved postage. Everyone will be happy.

A few people responded with enthusiasm, one person suggested I must have dementia and some chose not to answer. I suspect most of those who didn't respond have taken me off their list, which accomplishes the same goal.

I boxed all the remaining items in my Present Closet, and mailed them to a friend in another state. She and I do not share the same gift list so I figure she's safe.

This year's Christmas is almost here, and so far I've received only two presents. I've eaten the cookies, but if you want some stationary, let me know.

FAMILY THANKSGIVING

The nights are cold, the leaves are down, and we're heading into the holidays. Now that I've become Unmistakably Old, I'm more philosophical about how these days are celebrated—not how we plan them, because we always plan well. My more accepting attitude has to do with how things actually work out on the day. We've had some memorable snafus, like the year we went to cousin Joe's one bathroom condo and the toilet backed up. Another year the dishwasher spewed soap all over the kitchen because someone had used Ivory Liquid instead of dishwasher soap.

"Because we were using good dishes and Ivory is supposed to be gentle."

Unlike many of the younger members in my large family who still believe in the Norman Rockwell version of family gatherings, I now expect some amount of mishaps, disagreements, and disasters. And because of my age, I no longer have to host the event, which is a large bonus.

It's always fun getting together and last week some of us gathered at my oldest daughter's—the organized one-- to plan this year's Thanksgiving dinner. There were six of us, including the granddaughter who is studying psychology. This semester she is taking a course called Group Dynamics and she announced at our planning meeting that a family gathering is exactly like any other group, and we would all profit from understanding the various roles necessary for a group to function well. "If we're all aware of what roles are helpful," she said, "it will be better." She failed to say better than what, but even with that omission, her comment about roles spread rapidly that evening through the various branches of the family. Three people complained that there were never enough rolls; one requested whoever was bringing the rolls should provide some without seeds for those with lower intestinal problems and Sam, who is six, requested cinnamon rolls.

"Some roles are necessary to get things done," she told us. "We call those the task roles."

I was trying to pay attention, honestly I was, but sometimes when she gets going, she can be a bit dry. I'm sure I only closed my eyes for a moment, but I think I must have missed something, because the next thing I knew two of my daughters were arguing about what ingredients to put into deviled eggs. Mustard, pickle relish, and olives were all contenders.

"Since everybody loves deviled eggs," a daughter-in-law interjected, "why don't you each bring your recipe. I think they both sound good."

"That," the psychology granddaughter said, "is a perfect example of a peace-maker role, one of the emotional roles needed in a group."

"Like being a suck-up," another grandchild muttered. I was thankful her voice was quiet, since I wasn't sure there was a group role if things turned physical.

After another few hours, we had a list that seemed to cover everything from chips and dip to two kinds of pie and a persimmon pudding with hard sauce. A son-in-law who worked for a wine distributing company was put in charge of bringing wine, and we had navigated the rapids of turkey vs. ham by agreeing to both. The location this year was decided based on who had the biggest Flat-screen. I look forward to the phone calls between now and then, adding, subtracting, and modifying today's plan. We're an active all-American family who believe it is our birthright to change things at will; all the while wishing things would never change.

"I'm glad I was able to help," the psychology student granddaughter said. "You can see why I'm going into this profession. It's so practical."

"*Hmmm*," I replied. I think *hmmm* is a wonderful answer. It's non-committal, non-judgmental, and it buys time to think of what, if anything, you want to say next. In this case I decided saying nothing more was the best choice. It didn't seem the moment to inquire if a course in self-insight was going to be scheduled for her next semester.

Oh, I did receive an interesting phone call this morning. It seems rolls had been left off the list.

TURKEY GANGS

When I think about turkey, images of Thanksgiving flash in my mind. I have memories of children tracing the outline of a hand, coloring each finger a different color for tail feathers while the thumb outline becomes the turkey's neck and head. I see a golden roasted bird on the family table surrounded by cranberry sauce, two kinds of potatoes and all the other special dishes. Turkey is the symbol of a warm and loving family tradition we, along with most of America, repeat each year.

But things have changed. This spring I've been introduced to the dark side of turkey life. Turkeys have invaded our neighborhood, and not just one or two. Turkeys, it turns out, travel in gangs and we've been selected as *turf* for four gangs.

"It's only a few birds," a granddaughter wrote me when I shared news of the invasion with her. I referred her to the Hitchcock movie to suggest there was no such thing as "only" when it came to bird invasions.

"Who's dog left this?" a daughter asked, which points to one of the problems wild turkey gangs create. When a dog leaves this type of mess, there is an identifiable person who will clean up. It's more difficult to find people who are willing to assume that role with turkeys since none of us invited the birds to our neighborhood.

My first approach in getting them to go away was to wave my hands and say *"shoo."* If any of you are facing this problem, I strongly advise you to avoid saying *"shoo."* Besides being incredibly noisy, turkeys are aggressive. While I've never been a member of any gang, I've read gangs are organized around dominance, the most aggressive bully turns out to be the gang leader. Clearly *"shoo"* was interpreted as a challenge to the turkey's position as leader.

As someone who is Unmistakably Old, I fancy myself resourceful when faced with a problem, so I went on the Internet to learn more about these unwelcome invaders. Knowledge, I told myself, will help us discover how to encourage them to move on.

"They change color to reflect their mood," I told my friend Mildred. "Red indicates they are in an aggressive state, either to fight a perceived threat of some kind, or to establish a connection with some cute girl turkey."

"So when you said '*shoo*', he turned red?" Mildred asked. "I'm assuming he thought you were challenging his leadership and not that he thought you were a cute girl turkey."

I nodded.

"Although..." she continued, but being kind, she stopped, and took a sip of coffee before switching to information about her cousin.

"My cousin John must have some turkey genes," she said. When he gets upset his head and wattle turn red. So what gets rid of turkeys?" she continued.

"Hard to say. I read they're afraid of coyotes, but as far as I know, we don't have any. Some company advertises coyote urine, but it turns out turkeys have a very poor sense of smell. Coyote urine seems a waste of our money. Even worst, it might cause other birds to avoid the neighborhood. Meanwhile, an entire gang flew onto my deck. I have no idea which gang it was, but there was a big tom, three lady friends, and what appeared to be a couple of teens. My granddaughter's two children were there."

"And?" Mildred was getting into the drama of the situation at this point.

"And her daughter Jilly who's four said we needed to put up pictures of the Pilgrims because that would scare them. Bobby, who's eight, was more practical. He pulled out his water pistol.

Not only is he a good shot, but turkeys dislike being shot with water. The gang leader turned bright red and they left as a group. I'm not sure this is a permanent solution, but it reclaims my deck until we can come up with something better. For now, Bobby and I have bonded as the fifth gang in the neighborhood. Our motto is *we're small but tough. "*

PRESIDENT'S DAY

Now that I'm Unmistakably Old, I've been told I should also be wise, so I'm trying to figure out how. My first thought is that a wise person could teach our children that honesty is the best policy. I mentioned the idea to several others who agreed. Next I began to wonder if honesty was talked about in schools these days. I remember being taught about our first president as a boy. He chopped down a cherry tree. When asked about the tree, we were told he said,

"Father, I cannot tell a lie. I chopped down the tree."

Let's begin with the question of why a young child was walking around with an axe. As we ponder that issue of poor parenting, we're told the entire story, designed to teach the value of honesty, was a fabrication—fabrication being another word for a lie. The story was concocted by a writer/bookseller who needed an appealing biography for a rather bland man. So then we need to deal with another reality. Our first president, George Washington, was boring.

To teach children to tell the truth, someone created a story that is a lie and this lie became an important part of the curriculum of American schools.

Even if we can't point to George, there's always Honest Abe. There are stories about Lincoln who, we are told, frequently walked great distances to correct mistakes he made in the store where he worked. What type of mistakes? He is reported to have given too little tea to one customer and too little change to another. While the reports fail to let us know how frequently these "mistakes" occurred, they emphasize the value of honesty. Unfortunately they also suggest that President Lincoln's math skills were, at best, slow and he also seemed to lack any consistency in paying attention to the details of weights and measurements. I would suggest these are hardly stories to provide motivation to today's future presidents who are expected to learn some basic math.

While stories of these two men were taught as fact when people my age were in school, there is some attempt now to suggest to children that they may be apocryphal. Still, no one knows how many classrooms are teaching a more accurate version of history. It is also difficult to know what teachers are saying to children who come to school and inform everyone their grandparent is quite sure the cherry tree story is fact.

There is also some confusion about President's Day itself. Children are now being taught it is a day to celebrate the birthdays of both Washington and Lincoln. There is an implication these are the only Presidents with birthdays in this month. As far as I can tell, while children are celebrating with pictures of cherries and top hats to say Happy Birthday Presidents Washington and Lincoln, there are few to no young voices saying Happy Birthday President Reagan! Happy Birthday President Harrison. I'm pretty sure there are no nationally recognized symbols for young children to color and take home for either man. Many of us remember President Reagan so we're in a window of opportunity to come up with something to fill in a few of those gaps for our grandchildren, but what about President Harrison? Surely a jug of hard cider, one of the symbols used during his campaign, would be inappropriate, but since he claimed Ohio as his new home, a buckeye might work. Perhaps the fact he became president and died thirty days later is enough. The problem is, some of the books report he died because he caught pneumonia on inauguration day, a cold rainy day when he was outside without his hat and coat. Unfortunately, this is another untruth. His illness didn't begin until more than three weeks after the inauguration and is now assumed to be from enteric fever, not pneumonia at all.

Maybe teaching young children the value of honesty isn't the best way to work on becoming a wise old person. Or perhaps it's trying to use Presidents to illustrate the virtue is the mistake. I'm off to get a latte to think this through. All I know so far is that becoming wise is not a simple task. And that's the honest truth.

MY HOLIDAY PARTY

Every December I give a sit-down dinner party for some friends, but this year I decided I'd give a different type of holiday party. No customary turkey and cookies in the shape of wreaths. No sliced ham or pineapple upside-down cake. No casserole buffet. Other people could be counted on to come through on the traditional, so I thought I'd provide a little variety. It took me some time to ponder what would be really different, but I finally came up with an idea I thought would be both interesting and fun. The invitations I sent included the following sentences.

"This is an hors D'oeuvres only party, and I'm inviting twenty people so we should have enough to eat. Bring your favorite hors D'oeuvres, but NONE can be made with either condensed soup or dry soup mix."

Let me tell you, all those words after the BUT made things interesting. Here are some of the responses.

"Don't you know the economy is still trying to recover? I like to use soup to help out the soup company, because Campbell stock is part of my retirement plan.

"I thought all Hors D'oeuvres were made with some type of soup."

"Is this one of those brain exercises that AARP says we should do?"

"If we have this many Hors D'oeuvres, won't people be too full to eat dinner?"

"You always were 'bossy'." (A comment from a younger cousin who I included as an afterthought.)

"Does that mean we're not having a main course?"

"How can I make my sour cream and onion dip if I can't use Lipton's Onion Mix? Do you have another recipe?"

"Could I bring the desert instead?"

And my personal favorite, from Carol. "Please reconsider the "only" part of the menu. Hors D'oeuvres are much better with wine."

I sent out a P.S. to the invitations. "Hors D'oeuvres are all we're having to eat, but punch and wine will also be served."

The early comments didn't seem promising, but perhaps my P.S. helped because nineteen of the twenty people showed up. Pat was the only no-show, an excused absence because her daughter went into labor that afternoon. However, she sent a crock-pot of delicious Swedish meatballs. Of the other nineteen, there were sixteen absolutely delicious dishes, one so-so and one pretty bad. The bad one was made by Gladys and everything she cooks is terrible.

The nineteenth was a plate of cookies, brought by Sylvia who, when someone asked why she didn't bring an Hors D'oeuvres like everyone else, said she wasn't sure what that was, so she brought cookies because everyone likes cookies. No one pursued the conversation, but we all knew she was lying. The truth was she simply forgot.

The party was a huge success and next month we're planning a desert only party at Mildred's—with wine and coffee of course. Carol volunteered to call and remind Sylvia. I'm debating between a chocolate moose cake I make every Christmas and my special lemon meringue pie. I did hear Gladys called to ask if condensed soup could be used in the desert.

CHRISTMAS CHANGE

Have you noticed the amount of change around us? Of course we all know about the technology revolution and most of us try to keep up at least a bit—a cell phone here, a computer there.

But for some reason this Christmas season, the enormity of how different things are in all aspects of our lives has hit me, beginning with how scattered family members have become, many too far away to come home for Christmas. I think the change happened slowly so it was well underway before some of us noticed.

Now there are so many differences that I feel quite dizzy with it all. For example, I was surprised to learn how many families no longer hang up stockings. I used to needle point stockings for each new family member, only to learn stockings are seldom pulled out from the Christmas box in some of my descendant's homes. It's amazing to me how they expect Santa to come with no stockings hung by the chimney with care.

More than half of my relatives have shifted to fake trees, some with permanent lights. *"Good for the environment"* I'm told. I'm skeptical. I read articles about how difficult it is for plastic to break down, once it arrives in landfill. The other problem with plastic is the lack of pine smell, but that's not really a problem because the scent now comes in a can or a candle.

I've also noticed a few relatives have moved away from red and green in favor of designer ornaments. One niece has a white plastic tree decorated in purple ornaments. It's lovely looking but it's not very *"Christmas"*.

And don't even get me started on what appears on most tables pretending to be Christmas dinner.

As a family member who is Unmistakably Old, I've earned the right to be a member of the *"I remember when"* Club.

- I remember when the Christmas colors were red and green.

- I remember when popcorn was strung and paper chains were pasted to decorate trees along with the ornaments tenderly saved from year to year.

- I remember when we saved the wrapping paper for next year and even ironed the few crumpled pieces.

- I remember when Christmas decorations never went up before December and a special treat was to go downtown to see how the stores decorated their windows.

- I remember when baking and decorating cookies, steaming pudding and making fruitcake filled the house with Christmas smells.

- I remember when someone read *The Christmas Story* and *The Night Before Christmas* every Christmas Eve.

Some or all of those things have given way to what is fast, convenient, and up-to date. However, I know this as well. I know time blurs the hard edges of reality, blunting the difficult and glorifying the good. I know Christmas still caries the message of love and peace, even if it arrives in plastic. And I know when the current generation of children become Unmistakably Old, they will have their own warm memories, perhaps of purple ornaments on white plastic trees.

So here's what I'm planning to do. I'm going to bake something---probably krumkake. I will ask one of my offspring to bring me a bit of pine, which I will make into a table decoration with red and green ornaments along with some pinecones and I plan to read *The Night Before Christmas* along with *The Christmas Story* to any and all who care to listen. And I will remember it is people, not decorations, who make Christmas warm and safe.

Just thinking about this has gotten me into the Christmas spirit.

And so, to all of us, old and young,

"Merry Christmas to all and to all a good night."

THANKSGIVING

Where I live we have wild turkeys walking around. They are lean, aggressive, unattractive birds and I wonder who first got the idea to eat them. I know the story about the Indians and Pilgrims coming together for this great fall feast and since we've been told the Indians were experts on corn and fish, I'm assuming one of the Pilgrims was responsible for the turkey.

I'm trying to imagine the reaction of his wife or mother when he walked in with this dead bird and presented it to her with instructions to remove the pinfeathers before cooking. That was the era when wives and mothers were given instructions and, I gather, followed them.

I'm also having a bit of trouble imagining the reactions of those at the first Thanksgiving when everyone sat down and viewed this mixed assortment of food. Surely this tough sinewy bird, even minus pinfeathers, couldn't have commanded center stage. But codfish, prepared in any way they might have tried, strikes me as wrong. I know cranberries grow in Massachusetts so there might have been cranberry sauce, which always helps turkey. I'd guess there was no relish tray but perhaps gravy?

At our Thanksgiving dinners, gravy is always a dish requiring multiple refilling so I'm hoping there was enough at that meal because I'm not sure which language was used, or even what language the Wampanoag tribe spoke and we English speakers are pretty insistent others speak our language. How would you imagine someone at the table would pantomime needing more gravy if the hostess didn't notice the gravy bowl was empty?

Our elementary school books present this first gathering as a relaxed happy party, bringing together good friends to celebrate a good harvest. This idea is what most of today's families are trying to recreate. I don't want to be a spoilsport, but there is some misunderstanding here. The actual purpose of the gathering was business. In fact, the Pilgrims were attempting to negotiate a treaty of some sort. So, besides being a model for future Thanksgivings, this get together was, apparently, the first example of how to conduct a business luncheon.

What I don't know is the role of sports in the day's activities. Of course there was no television, but one of our former Presidents demonstrated that it was possible to have everyone run outside into the yard and begin a game involving some ball. My impression of the Pilgrims is they were a serious lot who wouldn't own a ball, much less have an amateur team for the year's sporting event. The Wampanoag, on the other hand, had been living in the neighborhood for at least several generations. It's possible they may have had a history of sports, although probably not football. Perhaps, as polite guests who were attempting to get into the spirit of the day, the Wampanoag didn't press the issue.

In our family, Thanksgiving dinner ends with pie. It's likely that both the Pilgrims and Indians would have known about pumpkin, although I doubt, under those living conditions, the pie crust would have been very flakey. When I was in Massachusetts, however, I was served something called Indian pudding, a desert made from corn. I wasn't very fond of it, although the people I was traveling with thought it grand. They ordered it with vanilla ice cream and the ice cream improved the dish. Maybe my friends' fondness for the desert indicates they're descended from some of the originals that attended that first dinner party. Still, I'm not at all sure where either Pilgrims or Wampanoag would have found vanilla ice cream.

V. TECHNOLOGY

"Technology involves a new language and new customs. It occurs to me that transforms us into immigrants without any need to leave home. I'm not sure if we're illegal"

An Unmistakably Old Woman

1. APPS
2. EMAIL OPPORTUNITY
3. FRIENDING
4. HI-TECH
5. YELLING
6. GIVING UP THE CAR KEYS
7. TOILET PAPER

APPS

Those of us who are "Unmistakably Old" grew up in a non-computerized world. Learning new concepts and skills, while possible, isn't simple. Add to this the fact that many of us are somewhat forgetful, and almost anyone could predict a pile of tech disasters littering the highways of the elderly.

Still, most of us go back for more. We've discovered that without leaving the comfort of our home, we can shop, send greeting cards, read books, play games, pay bills, do our taxes, find a new way to cook fish, and chat with friends and relatives anywhere in the world. Anything we might want to do apparently has an App.

Since these facts seem obvious, I fail to understand why whoever works in this field isn't more "tuned-in" to our age group. All the publicity I've read indicates these "geeks" are creative, smart, even brilliant young people. Their promises for what each new program will deliver are tempting. Most of the programs, however, lack the *"User-friendly for the Unmistakably Old"* seal of approval.

Yesterday I downloaded a new app. When I clicked on, I found myself on the *downward slope to you know where*, although at the beginning I didn't realize.

"Please enter your User ID and password" appeared on my screen. I did and was told one or the other was incorrect.

"Which one?" I questioned.

"The information is incorrect," the screen said. I modified the User ID and clicked enter. *"Your User ID or password is incorrect,"* the screen repeated. I tried a different password, then another. *"Your User ID or password is incorrect."* I tried another password and clicked *Enter*, only to be told I couldn't have another guess, and it was pretty clear I was guessing. I could, the screen advised, ask for help if I'd forgotten. I clicked

and learned they would email me an answer.

However, with all the back and forth, my mail seemed to have disappeared. I returned to the incorrect message screen, found an icon that would allow me to have a new password and read the rules.

- Do not use a password you have used within the past year.
- Include both upper and lower case letters and numbers
- Do not repeat the same letter more than 3 times

The only rule I thought I might have trouble with was the first, since my memory isn't terrific, but I thought I'd hope for the best. I made up a new password. The screen then said,

"We need some security information. Please select and answer one question from each of the following four categories."

The questions in each category were a collection of references relevant to the young, but not my generation. I passed over the name of my first concert, an event yet to occur, in favor of where I had my first kiss. Since my parents have been gone a long time, I reasoned I couldn't get into trouble for that one. And I wrote down each question and answer—a precaution needed because of the memory thing. It seems to have worked because the box wanting a password had disappeared, my mail had returned and, although it had taken three hours, I was back to the original screen where the new App happily sat.

I looked at the screen, debating. If I clicked, there was a 50/50 chance I would get to where the app promised to take me. The other 50% promised to have me spend the next three hours with the identity/password and security game I had just been through. It took me just one minute to decide to close the computer and pick up the telephone, which worked without security questions, ID or password. The call was a success. My computer-sophisticated grandson is coming on Saturday and that's soon enough to check out the new app.

EMAIL OPPORTUNITIES

I was beginning to feel quite relaxed with the idea of using the Internet in spite of the frequent warnings about hackers. "They can steal your identity," I'm told by my more cautious friends. I suppose that's true. However, I've always comforted myself with the idea that I'm in a large pool of potential victims and my individual identity isn't very interesting.

As a consequence of technology, it seems to be true that once a person is on the Internet, everyone is able to know almost everything about them. So I've always assumed my educational background and accomplishments (or lack there-of) are a part of common knowledge. I also assume my gender, date of birth, ethnic background, marital status and the number of my children and grandchildren are also part of common knowledge. Which means, everyone knows that I am, among other things, Unmistakably Old.

So you can understand why I was shocked when I received an invitation through my email to apply for a grant to further my education. "*This will allow you,*" the message said, "*to make more of a contribution to society. When that occurs, you will find your sense of self-worth and personal happiness will increase.*" Apparently technology wasn't able to let them know I was already happy.

I was still puzzling about that message, when a second offer came. This company wanted to train me for a new career where I could work from home. The at-home part seemed manageable at my age, but I'm not sure I want to start a new career.

I also received three different offers by a company who wanted to find me a job. Apparently this company thinks I have a sufficient amount of training or education, although I didn't open their offer to see what type of job they felt I could handle.

As a result of these emails, I tried to think how I had given the impression I had too much time on my hands or too little money to continue to survive. Maybe a descendant who's not in my will put my name on a "needs a job" site.

I was still pondering this when I opened my email to find an offer to improve a part of my anatomy I don't possess. Later the same day there were three different offers from exotic female names promising I'd be pleased if I opened their email. I deleted those on the spot since I have at least one grandson who I'm sure would be pleased to open their sites and he was coming over that evening to help me with a technology problem.

Perhaps someone figured out I was old, because yesterday there was an invitation to click on and join the growing number of lonely over fifty adults who are searching for companionship and love. I'm neither lonely nor searching, but I'm beginning to understand that Internet marketing is random.

So, in spite of how everyone's personal information, including mine, is available to one and all, there are many who don't bother to look. These apparently include providers of high school and college degrees, career training programs, hiring and job placement businesses, Republicans, Democrats, non-profit agencies, scam artists and those in the romance trade. With so much random incompetence, I think I'm safe.

FRIENDING

At some point on my way to Unmistakably Old, people began changing our day-to-day language. Perhaps language change and the addition of new words has always occurred, but it seems to be happening so rapidly that parts of today's English sound almost like a foreign language, at least to those of us who are old. The part of this trend I'm having the most difficulty with is how previously solid nouns are being turned into verbs. My example of the day is the lovely noun *friend* that is now also a verb called *friending*.

I try to keep up, especially with things on the computer. That was the reason I signed up for a Facebook account and I have friended and been friended by people of all ages.

I check my computer and Facebook account daily, and of course I have a routine. Each morning when I wake up I pour myself a cup of coffee, take the cup to my desk and turn on the computer. Last Tuesday was no exception. As I clicked on to see if any monumental changes might have occurred during my sleep, I was greeted with the following.

3 PEOPLE HAVE UNFRIENDED YOU - This is not a good way to begin a morning. Next to those words was a button to click to identify these 3 people. Many of you will not be surprised by what happened next. The button to "*connect here to see who*" did not connect. Instead the unfriended message somehow disappeared.

Now I've always believed if there is a problem you either do something, or you let go, a fix-it or forget-it philosophy. Since friendship is important to me, I chose the fix-it alternative and called one of my granddaughters. Fortunately she was available and came over after work. She spent some time on my computer before announcing she couldn't find anything about my being unfriended and it was probably a mistake. I felt better since this granddaughter is quite sophisticated when it comes to computers. Still, the thought lingered.

"Stop worrying," I repeated to myself, attempting to speed my journey into forget-it land. I did ask around. No one I contacted had an unresolved problem with me, and none had been unfriended themselves. I couldn't decide if that information made me feel better or worse.

A week passed and I was making progress toward letting the issue fade away. I did worry just a tiny bit as I was going to sleep two nights ago, but other than that, I didn't give it much thought. Until this morning! I woke up, took my coffee to the desk and turned on the computer. There, in black and white was the message.

10 PEOPLE HAVE UNFRIENDED YOU. I'm sure you know what happened next. I clicked on to the "find out who" button and the message disappeared. Nothing I did after that produced any helpful information. So this is my appeal. Did you send the message? Do you know who did? Are you part of a group who no longer wants to be my friend? If any of those questions fit for you and you would like to talk about it, please feel free to contact me. I always have energy to connect with friends and work through most problems or misunderstandings.

In the meantime, however, I'm definitely moving into the forget-it category. I've decided the idea of spending time worrying about something described by a word that didn't exist until recently is a complete waste of time and energy. And by the way, if you'd like to be my friend, I have room.

HI TECH WORLD

I received an email from my credit card company asking me to answer a questionnaire. *It will only take a few minutes of your time* they said. Answering did not take a few minutes. It took a half-hour, which is excessive. At this stage of life every hour is precious and I don't like giving half of one away.

The gist of what they wanted to know was what could they do to convince me to handle my account with them online. They asked, offered, and implored before presenting multiple choices to explain my "NO!" *Why* they wanted to know, but none of their choices fit my reason, which was: *the number of tech things I currently deal with has left me exhausted.*

Even clocks are no longer simple, especially those clocks built into other things. They work, according to my grandson, on a chip and part of a chip's nature, when it becomes upset, involves flashing. My clocks flash. My oven clock flashes. My microwave clock flashes. My coffee maker clock flashes. It seems no matter how many times I reset these clocks, something happens. The strange part is they all flash 12:00. I wonder why some of my clocks don't choose a different number? They could flash their favorite hour – even a clock must have a favorite.

I've asked several people to explain this preference clocks have for 12 but the only one who even attempts to answer is the same grandson who is now an unemployed dot-com person. From the complexity of his answer, I can understand why tech stocks got into difficulty. I'm just happy I don't have a seizure disorder since I understand flashing lights can trigger a seizure.

Many of my appliances, including my oven, microwave and bread machine, have chips allowing them to start doing whatever they do without my being around. I could come home from an afternoon at the movies to find my dinner, complete with freshly baked bread, warm and waiting for me. I don't think there is a chip that knows how to set the table, but maybe I've overlook something?

Then there is my self-cleaning oven, programmed by a keypad, and an induction cook top that can be programmed more easily by my cat walking across it than by me. When I counted there were eleven different keypads involved just to run my kitchen. I'm glad I have only myself to feed since on days when things seem too complicated, I'm happy with a bowl of corn flakes.

I recently replaced my heating/ air conditioning system and this new, energy efficient model functions on a keypad, which I've pretty well mastered. On the other hand, my entertainment center is complicated enough that some nights I choose not to be entertained, and my security system is such a computerized nightmare that I am thinking of replacing it with a Great Dane. The garden is watered by a computerized automatic sprinkler system, the telephone independently answers and takes messages and the FAX will remember the message if I forget to put in paper. My car doors open and lock with a tiny computerized keypad that is convenient except for a little button marked PANIC. Once PANIC is pressed, the car then makes a lot of noise, causing the owner, in this case me, to begin to experience PANIC.

We are told that all of this is designed to make our life easier, but I'm not so sure. I can remember the days when everyone knew a chip was something you ate and you couldn't eat just one.

So, credit card company, this is my answer to *why*. If you want my continued business, you'll have to accept my check.

YELLING

Someone, some time ago, told me using all upper case letters in a computer generated document was yelling, and therefore rude. This was helpful information since those of us who are Unmistakably Old don't always know the latest manners for technology.

I have discovered, however, that YELLING and therefore UPPER CASE WRITING does have a place. I've developed some guidelines I'd like to share with you.

Remember the old days before every child had his or her personal cell phone or mobile device? When it was time for dinner, most of us stuck our head out the kitchen door and yelled BOBBY and Bobby knew it was time to come home. In our neighborhood it was only Pete who needed repeated yells and never responded until his mom escalated to PETER ALAN HAYS. Well, there are people, actual adult people who, for whatever reason, seem to be so oblivious that yelling is all that gets their attention. Once they are yelled at most of them are sorry and offer excuses like, "*I've been so busy*" or "*My water heater broke.*" Personally, I think they are all friends with Peter Alan Hays.

Then there are people who have a difficult time paying attention. My granddaughter, the one who's studying psychology, is always telling me about these new fangled diagnoses they are coming up with to explain children's behavior, and I suppose in some cases this is helpful. But there is also something called "mother deafness" that occurs in most children around sentences like *Please clean your room today* or *The garbage needs to be taken out.* It is those situations where graduating to yelling seems to work.

Now those children are adults and I no longer care if they clean their rooms or take out their trash, but I do care about being informed about changes in plans and other things that impact me. "*I forgot*" and "*I thought you knew*" only works once-maybe twice-and then YELLING is appropriate as far as I'm concerned. After all, it's not like anyone can say, "*I tried to call, but your line was busy.*" As far as I know, it's not possible to get a busy signal on email.

Whether to yell back when someone yells at you is tricky. Some relationships seem to do OK with periodic yelling back and forth. No one gets too wounded and everyone seems to feel better when the air is cleared. There are other people who become very upset with yelling, and whether it's on the Internet or in person, would never raise their voice. Most of us are somewhere in-between, so I don't have a rule here.

What about YELLING for emphasis? Yes, if not overused. Here it's a little like swear words. There are times when *gosh, golly* just doesn't quite convey the feeling, and with email, the reader doesn't have the advantage of seeing your face or body language to help with the emotional context. On the other hand, if either swearing or yelling is part of your regular vocabulary, it takes away the impact.

So, there are times when "I'm REALLY upset" comes closer to conveying the feeling of frustration when the flowers you ordered for your best friend's anniversary party were delivered to the funeral parlor with the banner "Congratulations! We're Happy For You" in bold letters. And yes, that really happened. The friend's anniversary arrangement said "Our prayers are with you on this sad occasion." Fortunately these were good and lifelong friends and today we can laugh about the mix up, although I have no idea how the poor widow handled the Congratulations banner.

My point here, perhaps, is that absolutes usually get us into trouble. At least most of the time. Well maybe.

GIVING UP THE CAR KEYS

When my generation was raising children, we read a lot. It was the beginning of the era of *how* to books.

The children must have noticed we were reading about *how to handle them,* because they are now reading articles on *how to handle us.* Recently I noticed an article on *How to get the car keys away from mom or dad.*

Now of course there are some seniors who should no longer be driving, but not as many as the proliferation of articles would imply. This exaggeration of the danger may be payback for all our attempts to convince those children to eat broccoli.

Or maybe the writers are targeting a large number with the hope they'll be successful with a percentage of us. Their success may be lower then expected however. What the article authors are forgetting is how experienced my generation has become, as we raised our children, in resistance and subterfuge. We're not giving up those keys without a valiant fight.

My own children often lobbied for the car with the argument that they are safe drivers and are getting maligned unfairly. Any mishap they insisted was someone else's fault.

This is my argument now, but I'm not making things up that aren't real. I have additional evidence on the source of senior driving problems. A great percentage of today's seniors are not suddenly forgetting how to drive or loosing our skills and becoming bad drivers. The fault resides with the car companies. I believe many of the senior driver accidents are caused by changes in car design. Car companies now employ designers and engineers who are doing everything they can to make driving difficult for the elderly. It's called technology. Technology in automobiles is dangerous. Car salespeople maintain just the opposite, but we all know the reputation car salesmen have for honesty.

For example. There have traditionally been two reliable ways a driver could orient herself and avoid things like trees, fences and other drivers. These orienting devices were fenders and hood ornaments. In today's cars, the fenders are not visible to the driver of average height, much less those of us who are growing shorter. As for hood ornaments, they have completely disappeared.

Replacing those two is a camera and a television screen on the dashboard. These are part of the new technology designed to tell the driver a series of things, including what is behind the car when it's time to back-up. We are not just being asked to discard our own judgment, but to rely instead on devises never, before recent times, installed in a car. How stupid is that?

Back-up was exactly what I wanted to do one day last week since that was the only way to exit the driveway. Even though the gearshift is in a different place than it's always been, I've adjusted to that change so I put the car into reverse. Then, instead of turning to look where I was going, I focused on the computer screen built into the dashboard. Lines appeared and I stared carefully, trying to remember if the outer set of lines represented the distance I had left or if that was where an obstruction resided. The meaning of the graphic required more study, which I intended to do when I returned from the store, so I reverted to what I knew how to do. I turned around to look out the back window. At that moment the car began to beep at me.

"What?" I asked, not understanding the beeping. Clearly I was startled because then I accidently pushed some other button on the steering wheel.

"How can I help you?" a voice asks from the dashboard. Of course that startled me and I accidently hit the accelerator. Because the car was still in reverse, it shot backward. I slammed on the brake, which demonstrates how well my reflexes are working and the car stopped before I reached the street.

I looked out the rear view mirror and noticed a young man in a pick-up truck staring at me as he drove past my driveway. I'm pretty sure the hand signal he gave me isn't the one they teach in Driver's Ed. But I'm a nice person so I wave, then go back to figuring out how to get out of the driveway. I need groceries and I'd like to be there and back before any of my adult children show up to inform me I need to think about giving up my keys.

The next day I was explaining this to Mildred to illustrate how none of this was my fault. "The fault" I explained, "rests with those engineers at the car company, but you just know if I had hit the mailbox or that man's truck, someone would blame me."

"I see what you're saying," she responded. "But whether it's because of technology or something else, you're still the driver, so I can't see why an accident, if it occurred, is the car company's fault."

Even though she had a point, her remark made me cranky. Life's difficult enough when a person is old without complicating things with logic.

TOILET PAPER

"I'm investing in toilet paper."

Mildred was placing a third square of butter on her pancakes. I was ignoring the butter since I've figured my lecturing about the dangers of *bad fat* and *sodium* is not an effective deterrent.

"Is this about your idea that all old people have too much toilet paper?"

"No. I'm talking about an actual investment."

"Which company?" she asked." Is one of the manufacturers getting ready to declare a dividend?"

"I'm not buying stock," I answered. "I'm buying toilet paper. You should too. The technology is already there."

That produced the *look.* "I'm guessing you're going to tell me what you're talking about."

"Yes. Companies are going to stop making it. Toilet paper will soon be a thing of the past, like roller skate keys and Super 8 home movies. And of course it will be replaced by technology."

"Where on earth did you hear that? You're making it up."

"It's true. AARP ran an article talking about all the things that are disappearing or are going to be disappearing. They said so. There was also an article in the New York Times.'"

"Toilet paper?" She was so distracted by this news that she began to eat her pancakes without putting on any more butter.

"So what are we supposed to do? I mean, what else could we use? People must have used leaves or something, back in the old days, but how could that work for city people. A tree could get stripped of its leaves in a week if everyone in a big apartment building only had one tree to rely on. And you know some people would start hoarding leaves. Technology? Maybe robots?"

"There's a new kind of toilet," I told her. "With the push of a button it will spray you with water and blow-dry you. There are places in other countries where they already use those toilets. A company in Japan manufactures them."

Mildred was in stun mode, staring at me. "How long do we have?" she asked. "I just had my bathroom redone. No one said anything to me about a new kind of toilet."

I don't expect it will happen overnight," I answered. "Maybe they'll still have some regular toilets during our life time. But I figure a lot of people will think it's a great idea. Just like people think laptops and cell phones are a great idea."

"So you're trying to stock up? How do you know how much can you use over the next years?"

"It's not just for me. It's part of my long-term plan. I think there are going to be a lot of people who will react like you did. They aren't going to want to give up the idea of toilet paper either. So I'm planning to sell toilet paper to those who refuse to modernize. Since no one knows what's going to happen with Social Security, this is my income supplement plan. If you want, we can go into partnership."

She sat quietly for a moment, and then looked up, on the verge of saying something.

"Wait," I said. "Don't give me an answer this morning. You need to think it over, and in the meantime, it would be helpful if you went onto the computer and did a little research about prices and brands."

"And what are you planning to work on?" she asked.

"Storage," I answered. We'll need a lot of storage space and neither of us have much extra room. I mentioned it to my oldest daughter, but that didn't work out too well. She has the space, but she kept mumbling something about dementia."

Mildred sat, shaking her head.

"We have to be proactive," I said.

"I suppose," she answered. "But I regret I ever took a stand against drugs. We should have left all those geek children alone—let them smoke pot. Maybe we'd never be in this technology world."

"We don't know the geek children were the ones who wanted to smoke pot. Maybe that was other kids."

She went back to adding butter to her pancakes. I didn't have the heart to discourage her.

VI. CHANGING VALUES

"Someone changed the rules when we weren't looking."

An Unmistakably Old Woman

1. **TAKING CLASSES**
2. **THE GYM**
3. **HOARDERS**
4. **HAVING WORK DONE**
5. **FOREVER YOUNG**
6. **WHAT'S IN A NAME?**

TAKING CLASSES

It seems there is a frenzy of "class taking" these days. At my quilting club last week, every member was enrolled in at least one class. Gladys was enrolled in three. Since Gladys is the worst cook in our group of friends, I didn't know what to think when she told me two of her classes were "cooking."

"WOW, How great," I said in the most supportive tone I could muster. "What kind of cooking are they teaching you?" I was hoping to hear something like "Basic Food Preparation" or "Simple Healthy Cuisine" so I was unprepared for her answer.

"One is called *Sushi-Making* and the other is *Unique Chocolate Dishes*. Last week in the chocolate class we learned how to mix melted chocolate with corn flakes for a really tasty treat."

Not wanting to hear details of any recipe combining corn flakes and chocolate, I asked, "What is your third class?"

"Japanese."

"Japanese what?"

At that point my friend Mildred gave me one of her *looks*. She told me later my voice was beginning to take on an edge. At the time, however, I thought Mildred might have indigestion. In all fairness to me, her indigestion produces almost the same *look*.

Apparently I was *on a roll* with my questions because I kept going. "You're taking Japanese because?" I asked. I immediately knew this was unanswerable for Gladys. She does things for reasons most of us don't understand and doesn't understand *why* questions. But in true Gladys style, she keeps the conversation going.

"Japanese is a difficult language," she said, "so it's going to take me a few years to actually become fluent."

I jumped on her new direction. "Can you say anything yet?"

"*Kon'nichiwa* which means hello and *Arigato* which means thank you. Those are both important words. The Japanese are very polite people."

"Yes, I've heard that, although I don't know any Japanese people."

"Me either, and of course that's too bad. Once I've learned the language, I'm sure things will change."

I didn't ask why, which shows some level of self-control on my part.

"This month I'm working on learning food names so I can order in restaurants."

Which is a *sort-of* sensible answer, although every Japanese restaurant I've been to provides both pictures and written English translations on the menu. Hoping there might be a logical connection a few sentences away, I kept going.

"Learning the Japanese for menu items is the reason for the class on fixing sushi?" A huge smile crossed my face. I'd done it! I guided Gladys through a verbal maze and we'd arrived at that point where the dots connected. But I had underestimated Gladys. She frowned, as if this connection hadn't occurred to her. Then,

"Well, I guess the class will be helpful, but I'm taking the sushi class so on some hot day next summer, when everyone is at my place, I can prepare dinner without needing to turn on the oven or stove. Dinner will be sushi and sun tea. Of course, the rice for the sushi needs to be cooked, but everyone is always asking what can they bring, so I figured I'd say, bring some sushi-rice. Isn't that a great idea?"

All I could think of to say was, "WOW!"

THE GYM

This year my family got together and gave me a single joint birthday present. I was excited. I'm always trying to downsize and one gift seemed a lot better than many. So, right after the birthday cake, my daughter handed me the present. I opened the card first, and inside was one of those little plastic things, like a credit card.

"Everyone contributed," a granddaughter said. "I've scheduled us for Monday afternoon, so I'll pick you up about two. Open the other package. It's what you should wear."

I won't bore you with the details of how spandex looks on a body the age of mine. At least only the shirt was hot pink.

The plastic card, it turns out, admitted me to a gym. Not a Low Impact Water Aerobics Class or a stretch to limber Yoga hour or a Senior Exercise program. It was a real towels and machines, "We Mean Business" place. I now understand the danger of not having a list to give relatives when they ask what you want for your birthday.

At a Gym, the women wear spandex in an amazing array of colors, although some of them shouldn't. Most of the men are walking around in sleeveless shirts I always thought were supposed to be white and used as underwear. One of those men, who looked too young to be employed, informed me his name was Matt and he was going to be my trainer. I had no idea what to do with that information, but I have a kind grandson named Matt so I was optimistic.

"I'll be on the elliptical," my granddaughter said, heading into a maze of black, twisted machines fitting the description for creatures from some science fiction movie.

"It's important to work on your core," Matt said, patting one of the machines. I didn't reply because I wasn't sure what my core was, and I thought it might not be an appropriate conversation with a young man I'd just met.

"What are your goals?" he asked.

I'm not sure he took me seriously when I told him, "Getting out of this place alive."

He hesitated, and then smiled as he wrote something on the paper attached to his clipboard. "We need an emergency contact name and phone number," he continued. I could hear loud grunts from a man trying to pick up some large metal bar. Not a single person was offering to help. "A contact name," Matt repeated.

"Why? What do you think is going to happen to me?"

"Probably nothing," he answered, smiling in an attempt to reassure me. The attempt didn't succeed.

I gave him the name and number of a daughter-in-law who is an attorney. I probably won't need legal back-up, but it never hurts to be prepared.

For the next hour Matt had me sitting, standing, squatting and lying on one machine after another, while he said things like "straighten your back" or "let's do another set." It was about as much fun as I remember childbirth, but with childbirth I had a baby when it was finished. After this hour I suspected I'd need a nap.

As we were approaching the end of our time, Matt walked me over to a huge ball, and instructed me to sit. That was when I rebelled. "I've seen this on television," I said. "I'm sure it's lots of fun, but I've had enough."

Matt started to argue, but apparently thought better. He probably wanted our relationship to end on a good note.

"Thank you," I said. "It was nice to meet you." I turned to walk toward the door to wait for my granddaughter when he said,

"It was nice to meet you as well. I'll see you Wednesday."

It turns out the present, encoded on my little plastic card, is a six-month membership, complete with an on-going trainer. Somebody in this family is out to get me. I have to figure out who before it's too late.

HOARDERS

"You're not going to believe this! Someone has come up with a new psychological problem."

"The holidays are stressful, so it's not a surprise," Mildred answered. "Anyone we know?"

"No, not a person, a committee and they don't have the problem—at least I don't know if they do. They've decided it's a problem for their patients or potential patients. It now has a name and it's in the book."

Mildred sat staring at me.

"Remember I told you," I continued. "Psychologists have a book where they list all the different mental illnesses. They're adding to it."

"How is your granddaughter?" she asked.

Whenever I say something of a psychological nature, Mildred assumes my granddaughter—the one who's studying psychology- has stopped by. Usually she's right, but not this time.

"I heard this on T.V. I'm pretty sure they're wrong."

"The committee's wrong?"

"I think so."

"And the people on this committee are psychologists of one sort or another?"

"Well, I don't know—the person on TV didn't say, but it's the official book they all use, so probably."

Mildred sighed, and then spread more butter on her toast, a technique she uses to avoid talking while she thinks. I've told her I'll give her time to think without the extra cholesterol, but she likes butter.

"What are they wrong about?" she asked before taking a bite of the toast.

"Hoarding. This committee has decided hoarding is a mental disease."

"Well, I've seen that program on television about people who hoard and they don't appear too healthy."

"Probably staged."

She continued eating her toast, which I interpreted as an invitation for me to keep going. "Well, maybe a few are real," I conceded, "but hardly enough to have a whole new category to apply to the general population."

The waitress refilled our coffee while Mildred kept eating the toast and watching me. She's always been good at doing more than one thing at a time.

"I think this label is part of the government's plan to turn the economy around," I continued.

Mildred put her toast down to focus her full attention on me. "How on earth" was all she said? It was a question that used to intimidate me when we were young. Now I'm used to it.

"There are a lot of us who save things for future use, so we don't need to continually shop. It's been years, for example, since I've bought rubber bands, plastic bags, refrigerator storage containers, even wrapping paper and ribbons. I don't have money to waste, but apparently, this ability I have to be frugal and live within my means is interfering with our country's economic recovery. As a result, I'm about to be labeled as a hoarder, and once that happens, *look out!* I become part of economic recovery."

She waited without saying a word.

"Once this idea catches on, some well meaning relative will whisk me off to a therapist who will diagnose me with this new category in the book. The diagnosis will trigger my insurance, one or more pharmaceutical companies will become involved, and the next thing anyone knows, housecleaners, recyclers, and Wall Mart will become part of my recovery. Multiply this by however many of us have been taught to *save and make* do and you can see the pattern."

Mildred signaled the waitress. "We're going to be here a while longer," she said to the waitress. "I'd like another order of toast and some extra butter."

HAVING WORK DONE

A group of us do things together. Last week we were having a wine and cheese get-together at Marge's house. When Sue walked in she announced she was having some work done the next morning. Gladys said it was about time because Sue's house was getting pretty shabby looking. Peg said she hoped Sue was changing the peach color on her living room walls because that shade of peach was outdated by the early 50's.

Of course there was a noisy discussion about shades of peach, as well as the value of homes that appeared lived in and comfortable versus homes where everything was modernized. During all of this, Sue was quiet.

"Who's ready for some wine? Red or white?" brought enough of a pause to hear Sue say, "I'm not having work done on my house. I'm having work done on me."

The reaction, after a moment of silence, was a volley of statements like *How exciting* and *Why on earth?* and *Tell us more.* Sue's work was going to be Botox for the area around her lips. At that point Doris confessed she'd had the flab in her upper arms removed a number of years ago, and Jan told everyone that before she started dating the man who became her current husband, she had a tummy-tuck. It was surprising how many of the group had "*work*" done. Pat's comment summed up the opinion of the loyal opposition, adding God to the mix.

"If God had wanted me to look 20 years younger than I am," she said, "He would have made me look that way."

Gwen responded, "If God had wanted me to look as old as I am, He wouldn't have invented plastic surgeons."

It was an early evening, partly because Sue wanted to get a good night's sleep before her *work*, and partly because something exciting was supposed to happen on one of the reality shows. Mildred drove this evening and on the way home she asked, "What do you think about this *having work done* thing?"

"I haven't given the idea much thought," I answered. Even though she was driving, I knew Mildred was giving me the raised eyebrow look. "And," I continued, "it's just as well. Plastic surgery is expensive."

"What if it were free?"

"Maybe. I wouldn't mind reclaiming a definite chin line. I look OK to myself when I look in the mirror, but when people take a picture of me and I see the side view--well, you know. And you? Would you have work done?"

She didn't hesitate. "Not on your life. I want to see me when I wake up and look in my bathroom mirror. A familiar face reassures me I'm still around. If another woman was staring back, it wouldn't be good."

And when I thought about her answer later, I thought she was right. Everything about her made her look like Mildred and any thing she did to change that ran the risk that she'd look like someone else. That would be a loss for us all.

FOREVER YOUNG

Now that I've become Unmistakably Old, I'm aware of the number of people who tiptoe around the word *old*. Yesterday I met one of my sons for lunch and the waiter called me *Young Lady*. While that's nonsense, I wonder what it would be like to be *forever young*. So far I'm not impressed with the prospect.

The experience, I imagine, would depend on which young age one selected. If I were in my teens, I might be stuck in a lifetime of pimples, homework, and teenage dates. Not appealing.

Or what about becoming *forever not quite that young*, say in my twenties? I was lucky during that decade. I found a great guy and settled down. But when I watch the members of my family who are currently in their twenties, life doesn't seem as easy as I remember. There are careers to launch, biological time clocks to worry about, and an economy gone wild. That's more stress than I want.

Perhaps a little older? There were wonderful days when the children were young. However, I also remember children fighting with each other, bedrooms that were never clean without serious parental threats, and late nights when I couldn't get to sleep until they were safely home. I remember the hysterical searching for lost homework papers, the tearful evenings when a boyfriend didn't call, and the catastrophe of the pimple appearing the afternoon before the prom. Those years held a lot of drama. I'm glad I did it once, but once was enough.

So what, I ask myself, are those people talking about? Maybe they think we miss getting up each morning to the shrill ring of an alarm. What about those cold dark mornings when you couldn't find your left slipper so you hobbled around with one foot on the icy floor.

Or maybe they think we miss the way things were done. Let's see. After the alarm and slipper routine, the morning started with bringing the milk in from the box outside the back door. The box was insulated so the milk wouldn't freeze, but the person first up had no such protection. It was necessary to move fast to bring in the milk and let out the cat while balancing on one slippered foot. Next was breakfast and doing dishes. The dishwasher was the same human who took out garbage, made beds, and mopped the floor. The fun had just begun. There was laundry, an activity where we pulled wet clothes from the machine, ran them through a ringer to remove excess water and then hung them on a line. The line was outside most of the year, but in the basement if the weather was too cold or wet. Almost everything needed ironing the next day. Rugs were *beat,* mattresses were *turned,* socks were *darned*, and everything was *slow cooked* because no one had invented fast food. Take-out meant a casserole you fixed for your sick neighbor. Now that I'm thinking about this, the lifestyle might have made us old.

Young was great when I was there. But that was then and this is now. Now I'm Unmistakably Old and so, when someone calls me young, I'm trying to decide what to do. It's a question of whether I consider them engaged in a misguided attempt to be nice or whether they're seriously demented. Unfortunately I'm no longer sure how to tell the difference so maybe I'll just look the other way. We know. Their day will come.

WHAT'S IN A NAME?

Have you noticed how uncomfortable people get about calling someone old?

I've been giving some thought to other ways to describe those of us who've lived longer than most. The focus is to find a word or phrase to communicate advancing age without offending anyone. My search has given me a new respect for people who come up with politically correct language. Finding alternatives isn't easy.

The first word I thought of was Senior. It's a popular label, with discounts as a primary attraction. There is a senior section on some restaurant menus. Movies, hotels and airlines offer senior rates although when I investigated, there were either serious restrictions on many offers or alternative ways to gain the same savings. It does however appear to be the most popular term, perhaps because it's endorsed by AARP, who also favor the word **Maturity**. One of my grandchildren overheard my conversation. She said,

"I think being a senior is awesome 'cause you get to graduate and move on."

Of course she is right, but for now I'm avoiding the label. I'll use the term when I get closer to the time I'm eager to move on.

One of my friends bought a home in a development catering to **Active Adults**, their designation for old people. After I discarded "senior" I spent the next week referring to myself as an active adult to see how it would feel. To tell the truth, I found it confusing. I've never been active, if by active they mean skydiving and the like. But I've always been active enough to have a busy life. Of course I was more active in my thirties than I am now. So, if I want to be honest, I guess I'd have to call myself *"a somewhat less active than before adult."* Too wordy! I

125

was also afraid the label might be reserved for residents of their community and I didn't want to move.

Next I tried, **Golden Agers,** even though I have no idea what it means. All I can think of is someone thinks we must have resources most of us don't have, and which Social Security isn't about to provide. Or perhaps there's something about it being the best time of life, a golden age, although I'm not sure I see it. I've decided it must be one of those old-fashioned sayings popular before my time.

By now I realized I was going to have to come up with an identifying word or phrase myself since the popular ones seemed inadequate. I gave the matter a great deal of thought and came up with **O Wise One**! I am quite excited. This designation for the oldest generation is descriptive, is earned with age, and shows an appropriate amount of respect. I plan to put on a strong campaign for its adoption once my family settles down. Laughing doesn't seem respectful. Until O Wise One achieves widespread popularity, however, I'm planning to stick with **Unmistakably Old**. It's accurate, if nothing else.

VII. RELATIONSHIPS

"My grandmother used to say, 'God gave us our relatives, but thank God we can pick our friends.' I don't think she was talking about me."
                              An Unmistakably Old Woman

1. **UNFINISHED BUSINESS**
2. **BEING HIT ON**
3. **PUD**
4. **COUGERS**
5. **THE "S" WORD**

UNFINISHED BUSINESS

Yesterday I had breakfast with my friend Mildred. The conversation was moving, as it often does, to the trials and tribulations of getting old, when she said,

"I've heard about what happens after we die. Once we get to Heaven, we have to resolve differences with everyone we've had unfinished business with during this lifetime."

"Unfinished business?"

"You know, hard feelings, misunderstandings, that kind of thing."

"Everyone?"

I ask short questions when presented with bad news.

"Everyone," Mildred answered, "even people from our past."

"This is what we do in Heaven?"

She nodded.

I pushed my plate of bacon away in the hope of preventing clogged arteries, thereby buying myself some extra time. This was sounding a little less Heavenly then I'd been led to believe.

What popped in my mind first was an argument I once had with a clerk over the price of some scarves. The sign said **SALE: 3 for $10**. I picked out three I liked, and went to the checkout counter where a young clerk, identified as Debbie on her nametag, rang up my scarves for $36.75.

"The scarves are on sale for $10," I said.

She looked up with a frown, and informed me that was impossible. "No one would sell scarves for that price," she said.

"There's a sale sign on the scarf table," I answered.

She accused me of untruthfulness. I invited her to go check. She asked me to either pay the bill or remove myself from the line. I suggested she call her supervisor. She... well you get the idea.

Eventually the supervisor became involved. The clerk was wrong on her pricing, but more important to me now was, although I got the scarves for $10, there were hard feelings. Unfinished business! I imagined she would be less than pleased to arrive in the afterlife to find me waiting.

"We have Unfinished Business," I'd say. I imagine her turning pale, although because she's dead, she might already be pale.

The issue with Debbie is only a beginning. A list of past arguments and misunderstandings began to form in my head. With my memory problems, the numbers could be far greater.

"Did you hear," I asked Mildred, "if Heaven supplies any staff to help organize?"

Mildred shrugged, which I didn't consider much reassurance since this is her idea.

"There's more," she said. "I've heard other people, ones we barely know, may have issues with us."

One-way unresolved issues? I pictured the scene.

"I didn't realize. I'm sorry."

"Sorry doesn't count."

"I didn't mean to hurt your feelings."

"But you did."

"What would you like me to do?"

"It's a little late, don't you think? After all, we're dead."

"Where did you hear this?" I asked. "Was it from someone reliable? Maybe they made it up."

"Maybe," Mildred answered. "We can't be sure."

I waited while the waitress refilled our coffee cups before asking, "Do you have any unfinished business with me that we need to clear-up?"

Neither of us did, which was nice. Still this idea has stuck with me. I know how good it feels to have issues with another resolved. Making sure all relationships reach that level would be

Heavenly. In the meantime I'm making a list of people I can talk to while I'm still here. I am having trouble locating Debbie. Seems the manager fired her some time ago, and he has no idea where she went. That means he also has unfinished business, but I didn't tell him.

BEING HIT-ON

"I was *hit-on* yesterday."

My friend Mildred looked up from her omelet. "Are you hurt? Who hit you?"

"No one hit me," I answered. "I wasn't hit. I was *hit-on*."

Silence and a frown.

"*Hit-on*," I said again. "It means someone made an advance, an exploratory comment."

Still silence, accompanied by a blank stare.

"It's an expression-a boy-girl thing- an 'I think you're sexy' type of thing."

"Some boy said you were sexy? *Really*? He said *sexy*?"

"Not a boy, a man. He didn't use those exact words. I don't know why that seems strange to you."

"What words did he use to make you think he found you sexy?" She took another bite of omelet.

"Never mind. I'll keep this news to myself."

"Nonsense," she continued. "I've just never heard this expression before. Must be something new from one of your grandchildren."

"I've always heard this. I heard it when I was young."

Mildred did the eyebrow look. "Well, you must have had a wilder youth than you've led us to believe."

It seemed better to not answer.

"Is there more to your story? Where did this *hitting-on* happen?"

"Church. He came up to me after service and began a conversation."

"A hitting-on conversation telling you he thought you were sexy, but without actually saying anything about sexy?"

"Right."

"Because it was in your church and saying sexy things wouldn't have been appropriate, but *hitting-on* was?"

It seemed time to move this conversation along since going around the *hitting-on* circle one more time didn't seem productive. "I called him," I said. "I got home and thought about it, and called him."

There are many reasons why Mildred is my best friend and at that point she demonstrated one. She remained silent, which is better than my oldest daughter—the up-tight one—managed to do when she heard. My daughter's comments circled through the usual dementia suggestions, built in intensity during a long speech about what her father would have thought of my behavior if only he were here and culminated in a lecture about my responsibility to set an example for the younger generation. It was one of her more impressive monologs, causing me to wonder once again where I had gone wrong in her upbringing, but that's a topic for a different day.

Back to Mildred. In a calm voice she asked, "What did you say when you called him?"

"Would you like to get a cup of coffee?"

"He said yes?"

I nodded.

"Have you had the cup of coffee yet?"

I nodded again.

"And? Is this serious? Is there something I should know?"

"Oh for heaven's sake! It's only the beginning of what may become a friendship. I've had one cup of coffee with the man. He isn't the problem."

"But there is a problem?"

"I read something upsetting last night."

"About him?"

"No. It was an article about how to behave when someone our age starts dating again. Imagine! As if a bunch of

Unmistakably Old women need advice. At this age it's stupid to be anything but real. If someone doesn't like that, tough."

"So I'll assume you were real? How did it go?

"It went well. We're going to the movies together tomorrow afternoon."

Then she got to the important question, the one she was pretending wasn't important.

"You're not planning to see one of the movies we have on our list, are you?"

Of course I said no. A guy can interfere with girlfriends during the teenage years, but not when one becomes Unmistakably Old.

PUD

"What have you been doing all week? You look awful."

Close friends who always tell you the truth are a mixed blessing. Mildred was a close friend.

"Baby sitting Cassie's dog PUD."

"She's a dog--an old dog. She eats, she sleeps, she goes out to do her business occasionally. So, why are you so tired?"

My friend Mildred is persistent.

"PUD snores."

This produced the raised eyebrow.

"She's loud," I continued. "Very, very loud."

"So loud you can hear her from your bedroom?"

"She was in the bedroom. Actually, on the other pillow."

"The reason she's in the bedroom is what? Why isn't she sleeping in your family room? That's where your dog slept before she died. You always said dogs don't belong in people's beds."

"She's in the bedroom because she howls."

"Excuse me?"

"Howls! I put her in the family room the first night. And she howled. Loud howling. Louder than her snoring."

"I see."

The waitress poured more coffee and took away my bagel plate. Mildred was still working on hers. She likes butter and cream cheese and lox, along with a bit of tomato and onion, placed on each individual piece. It's an *assemble and eat one piece at a time* ritual that I thought might give her a chance to consider the amount of cholesterol she was eating. When I mentioned that, she informed me that lox was salmon and salmon had fat put there to counter whatever else she was eating. She finished the bite she was working on. Then,

"Why don't you nap during the day?"

"I've tried. She opens doors. PUD doesn't like a closed door, at least if she's on the other side."

"She what?"

"She opens the door. You know how I have those lever handles on some of my doors? She knows how to push down on the handle to open the door. I can't even be in the bathroom alone."

"If I remember correctly, and you know I'm known for my excellent memory, your bathroom doorknob is one of those regular round ones."

"Yes, but on those doors, she knocks."

By now Mildred was staring at me as if this were some type of fabrication. "Honestly," I said. "I have no idea how she learned to do these things, but PUD refuses to be away from me if I'm in the house. She knows how to knock on the door. Persistently! I was in the bathtub and she started knocking.

"It's OK PUD," I said in my most reassuring voice. "Just lie down. I'll be out in a few minutes."

She kept knocking. I don't know how long that lasted--a long time--and then she started howling. I got out of the tub and let her in because I figured her howling was loud enough that she's was bothering the neighbors. Once she was in, she stretched out on the bathmat, fell asleep, and began snoring."

"Where is she now?"

"I left her at the house. I checked with Jean next door. When I'm gone, she doesn't howl."

"How much longer do you have PUD?"

"Another week."

Mildred shook her head in the way we all once did when we couldn't believe one of the children had, one more time, forgotten their homework.

"Well," she said. "I can't have you dropping dead from exhaustion. So here's what we do. I don't want to babysit PUD.

But you're welcome to nap in my guest room for the next week, on one condition."

"Which is?"

"The next time Cassie wants to travel and is looking for a sitter, you say no."

You can see why Mildred is such a good friend.

COUGARS

Have you heard about the new dating trend? Younger men and older women are hooking up. The women are called *"Cougars."* As someone who's Unmistakably Older and therefore potentially a candidate for one of these younger men, I decided the topic merited some thought. After all, if the opportunity presents itself, I don't want to stammer around, unsure of what to say.

To begin with, it's important to understand the young man's motivation. Some are probably looking for a mother. If that is the situation, one needs to take seriously whether teaching another male how to pick up their dirty socks, put the toilet seat down when finished, and wipe their feet before coming inside is worth whatever benefits may come from the relationship. Some of my friends say they are up for this challenge, but most of us have raised enough children and husbands.

While motivation isn't always easy to detect, I've discovered it becomes clearer if I utilize minimal conversation and maximum observation. An example would be "Please be sure and put the toilet seat down so I don't fall in some dark night and break my hip." That should be said only once, after which you observe to see if (a) he listens and (b) he remembers. Listening and remembering are key when determining whether he's a grown up. A clear pattern seldom develops before a month. If, after watching for that amount of time, you see that he has flunked, you're right in the middle of the *If I've told you once, I've told you a thousand times* syndrome, which we all recognize as mothering. The only remaining question at that point is "How do you feel about a broken hip?"

It's also important to discover if he likes to cook. Some women are delighted to find a new partner who is kitchen adverse or even incompetent, because they now have someone to cook for. I, on the other hand, believe the good Lord assigns to every woman at her birth a maximum number of dinners she must prepare for others. I reached my quota several years ago. Sure, I enjoy the occasional dinner party or holiday festivities, but a hungry, helpless person sitting nightly at my kitchen table would not only starve, but also get on my nerves.

Then there is the issue of whose friends you will spend time with. If yours, there is a definite advantage. Many of your cohorts will likely become inhibited and stop talking about their colons and gall bladders. That alone could make everything worthwhile.

On the other hand, if you hang out with his friends, interesting as they may be, there is the difference in energy level. The initial flush of a new relationship allows one to experience an amazing surge of energy. Trust me, it doesn't last. When the surge passes, you are faced with a partner who may like to dance or drink or party half the night, while you are yawning, and wishing for a soft bed. Compromise here is difficult. Dozing off can be embarrassing, especially if you snore.

In-laws are also a factor. Things get sticky when your new partner is younger than your youngest child, and your new mother-in-law doesn't yet need to color her hair. Those extended-family get-togethers may begin to take on the characteristics of an evening from Comedy Central as everyone stumbles around to find possible topics of conversation. Career changes? Easy recipes for after work dinners? Planning for retirement? Budgeting in retirement? Best clubs for dancing? The value of large print books? The demands of aging parents? How to have sex after a hip replacement? The possibilities for missteps are everywhere.

This whole idea of the older woman and the younger man is a relatively new phenomenon although we've always seen the reverse where older men seek out younger women. That's not called being a *Cougar* however. My friend Jessica, whose husband Herb divorced her for his young secretary, told me the term used to describe that behavior in men is *"Old Fool."* I don't know if she's right or not.

THE "S" WORD

One amazing gift of becoming Unmistakably Old is free time. Past a certain age people assume you're supposed to do little or nothing, exempting you from snide comments when you appear to be doing nothing. Recently, during my sitting around time, I began to think about sex, and came to realize that sex is one major surprise of old age. There is a general belief that once a person reaches the age of looking old, sex magically disappears from awareness. It is as if some internal delete button is triggered. Because that's what people believe, that's what they see, which of course allows those of us who appear old to have an enormous amount of undetected fun.

It is true there are changes that occur with the passage of time. No longer is sex an Olympic-qualifying event. At the same time it's important to highlight that sex remains a physical activity. Think about it! Sex, done right, accelerates heart rate, involves repeated stretching/contracting of muscles, and in general increases stamina. It amazes me it isn't a hot topic for geriatric fitness experts.

Timing is an issue for this activity. Sex at the end of the day is an age-old tradition, but evening sex is risky. Imprinted on the celluloid of our minds are images of candlelit dinners, a romantic glass of wine, followed by a fade-out to the bedroom. But as mature adults we have to face facts. Most of us can't stay awake, and a glass of wine is often as effective as a sleeping pill.

Another old rule that falls apart with age is the belief sex needs to wait until marriage. Now I'm as concerned as the next person about morality and commitment, and observing at least some of the societal rules, but facts are facts. The world is filled with single old people who, should they marry, give up one Social Security check. Social Security may not be what my grandchildren call *big bucks,* but it's important income for most of us. I can't think of any partner who's worth that much money.

Another outdated rule is, *Take your time getting to know someone, and don't appear too eager.* Perhaps taking time is a good idea at twenty but, once one has arrived at old, those who take their time stand a good chance of running out of time. Indian Summer is a short season.

Then there is the visual image. We old have arrived at the time of life when "moving south" is a description of the body's muscles rather than a search for a retirement community. If a muscle can sag, it has-- not a pretty sight. We need alternatives. Sex in the dark – sleep interferes. Sex with clothes on – one misses half the fun. Poor eyesight helps, but many older people still have 20/20 vision. Blindfolds are too kinky for many old people. Recognizing these superficial body changes are superficial is the only real solution. But until that happens, the following suggestions may help.

1. Begin by selecting a partner whose body has sagged further than yours so you can be generous-minded. In that way you set a tone of acceptance. And it's nice to be the best looking one in the room.

2. Avoid, whenever possible, the *on-top* position. The pull of gravity creates a bulldog effect on the facial muscles of the person looking down. Scary!

3. Even through it's probably daytime, choose a place with as dim lighting as possible. Curtains help. You can never count on a partner to keep their eyes closed. Most cheat!

No doubt about it, while age brings unique problems to work around, being old can be a real estrogen/testosterone whirlwind. So the next time you pass an old person who appears to be sitting, lost in thought, perhaps you'll give a little smile of encouragement.

CPSIA information can be obtained
at www.ICGtesting.com
Printed in the USA
LVOW11s1032060617
537108LV00003B/197/P